A Practical Guide to

Data Processing
Management

AUERBACH Data Processing Management Library

James Hannan, Editor

•

Contributors To This Volume

Jagdish R. Dalal
Manager, Management Information Systems, Brookhaven National Laboratory, Upton NY

Pat Duran
Consultant, Millis MA

Louis Fried
SRI International, Menlo Park CA

Al McCready
Manager of Information Systems Consulting,
Arthur Young & Company, Salt Lake City UT

Susan H. Nycum
Attorney, Gaston Snow & Ely Bartlett, Palo Alto CA

Paul M. Raynault
Computer Financial Incorporated, Hackensack NJ

William E. Sanders
Vice President, Management Information Systems, Ticor Title Insurers, Los Angeles CA

David Tommela
Assistant Manager, Information Systems, Southern California Edison Company, Rosemead CA

Robert E. Umbaugh
Vice President, Southern California Edison Company, Rosemead CA

Raymond P. Wenig
President, International Management Services Incorporated, Framingham MA

Larry D. Woods
Consultant, Moline IL

A Practical Guide to

Data Processing Management

Edited by James Hannan

AUERBACH Publishers Inc
Pennsauken NJ

VAN NOSTRAND REINHOLD COMPANY
New York Cincinnati Toronto London Melbourne

Copyright © 1982 by AUERBACH Publishers Inc

Library of Congress Catalog Card Number 82-11341

ISBN 0-442-20922-3

All rights reserved. No part of this work covered by the copyright hereon may be reproduced or used in any form or by any means—graphic, electronic, or mechanical, including photocopying, recording, taping, or information storage and retrieval systems—without written permission of the publisher.

Printed in the United States of America

Published in the United States in 1982
by Van Nostrand Reinhold Company Inc
135 West 50th Street
New York NY 10020 USA

16 15 14 13 12 11 10 9 8 7 6 5 4 3 2

Library of Congress Cataloging in Publication Data
Main entry under title:

A Practical guide to data processing management.

(Auerbach data processing management library ; v. 1)
1. Electronic data processing--Management. I. Hannan, James, 1946-   . II. Series.
QA76.9.M3P7   1982   658'.054   82-11341
ISBN 0-442-20922-3 (Van Nostrand Reinhold Co. : pbk.)

Contents

Preface			vii
Introduction			ix
Chapter	1	**DP Management: A Modern Challenge** Robert E. Umbaugh	1
	2	**Long-Range Planning** Louis Fried	9
	3	**DP Steering Committees** AUERBACH Editorial Staff	21
	4	**DP Policies and Procedures** Robert E. Umbaugh	29
	5	**Management Control Reporting** Louis Fried	53
	6	**Financial Alternatives for Computer Acquisition** Paul M. Raynault	67
	7	**User Chargeback** William E. Sanders	83
	8	**Problems in Decentralized Computing** Larry D. Woods	99
	9	**A Strategy for Systems Implementation** David Tommela	111
	10	**Selecting Software Packages** Raymond P. Wenig	127
	11	**Structured Techniques** Pat Duran and Al McCready	137

Contents

12 **Protecting Proprietary Interests in Software**
    Susan H. Nycum 147

13 **Security**
    Jagdish R. Dalal 157

Preface

In its relatively brief existence, the computer has emerged from the back rooms of most organizations to become an integral part of business life. Increasingly sophisticated data processing systems are being used today to solve increasingly complex business problems. As a result, the typical data processing function has become as intricate and specialized as the business enterprise it serves.

Such specialization places a strenuous burden on computer professionals. Not only must they possess specific technical expertise, they must understand how to apply their special knowledge in support of business objectives and goals. A computer professional's effectiveness and career hinge on how ably he or she manages this challenge.

To assist computer professionals in meeting this challenge, AUERBACH Publishers has developed the *AUERBACH Data Processing Management Library*. The series comprises eight volumes, each addressing the management of a specific DP function:

A Practical Guide to Data Processing Management
A Practical Guide to Programming Management
A Practical Guide to Data Communications Management
A Practical Guide to Data Base Management
A Practical Guide to Systems Development Management
A Practical Guide to Data Center Operations Management
A Practical Guide to EDP Auditing
A Practical Guide to Distributed Processing Management

Each volume contains well-tested, practical solutions to the most common and pressing set of problems facing the manager of that function. Supplying the solutions is a prominent group of DP practitioners—people who make their living in the areas they write about. The concise, focused chapters are designed to help the reader directly apply the solutions they contain to his or her environment.

AUERBACH has been serving the information needs of computer professionals for more than 25 years and knows how to help them increase their effectiveness and enhance their careers. The *AUERBACH Data Processing Management Library* is just one of the company's many offerings in this field.

James Hannan
Assistant Vice President
AUERBACH Publishers

Introduction

The extraordinary advances in computer and communications technology during the past 30 years have far exceeded our ability to apply and manage them in the business environment. This state of affairs is more a result of the dizzying rate of technological change than it is of benighted management; announcements of new and radically improved technologies are made with disquieting regularity. It is not surprising, then, that many of those charged with applying the computer in solving business problems have eagerly adopted new "solutions" and then searched frantically for appropriate "problems."

Although rapid technological change may, in large measure, account for the relatively underdeveloped state of data processing management, computer professionals themselves bear a good portion of the responsibility. Computing machinery has evolved well beyond the early electronic accounting machines that were wired and supervised by technical wizards to perform a limited number of applications for the company controller. Computers have changed, and the array of applications they support has broadened considerably.

For their part, however, computer professionals have been slow to make the transition from technical supervisor to business manager. All too often they have failed to develop the management skills needed to plan, implement, and manage the introduction and use of computers in their organizations. Instead of being the masters of the new technology, they have sometimes become its unwitting victims.

Thus the challenge for data processing managers in the eighties is to combine technical expertise with general management skills—to feel as comfortable in the upper management councils of their organizations as they do in the data center. This volume of the *AUERBACH Data Processing Management Library* is designed to help DP managers meet that formidable challenge.

We have commissioned an outstanding group of DP practitioners to share the benefits of their extensive and varied experience. Our authors have written on a carefully chosen range of topics and have provided proven, practical advice for managing the DP function productively.

In Chapter One, "DP Management: A Modern Challenge," Robert E. Umbaugh comprehensively surveys the challenges facing DP managers and discusses the types of training and skills needed to meet them.

Introduction

One very important management skill is the ability to develop a long-range DP plan that supports the organization's goals. In "Long-Range Planning," Louis Fried details the elements of such a plan and offers practical advice for developing a workable strategy.

DP steering committees have been a mainstay of many organizations for some 15 years. Because of the number of pitfalls associated with steering committees, however, few have succeeded. The AUERBACH Editorial Staff discusses the advantages and disadvantages of steering committees and describes a proven strategy for their successful implementation in Chapter Three.

While most DP managers recognize the importance of policies and procedures in enhancing control, promoting consistency in operations, and increasing productivity, few have taken the time to develop and publish such guidelines. Robert Umbaugh describes how to coordinate, administer, interpret, and introduce procedures in a DP installation in his "DP Policies and Procedures." He also provides practical guidelines for controlling the development of a procedures manual, including sample formats and development tools.

In addition to policies and procedures, the DP manager needs a way to measure DP performance if he or she is effectively to control the data processing function. To this end, Louis Fried proposes a comprehensive management control reporting system in Chapter Five.

Expenditures for equipment generally represent a sizable portion of any data processing budget. To allocate equipment dollars cost-effectively, the DP manager needs a thorough understanding of the various financial options available. In "Financial Alternatives for Computer Acquisition," Paul M. Raynault provides explanations and examples of the common alternatives to help the DP manager make informed financial decisions.

DP managers must also be mindful of the costs that arise from providing services to user departments. Chargeback systems offer a method of accounting for these costs. Designing and implementing such systems can be complex and have a significant impact on user/DP relations. William E. Sanders addresses the objectives of DP chargeback systems and offers a seven-step program for their implementation.

Even with an effective chargeback system, providing service to user departments can become problematic if applications backlogs begin to build. Users often attempt to circumvent backlogs by installing their own mini- or microcomputers. In "Problems in Decentralized Computing," Larry D. Woods discusses the many problems that stem from user independence and recommends that the DP and user departments adopt a cooperative approach.

Perhaps the most effective way to obviate user impatience is to shorten the chronically lengthy development times for new applications. In his

Introduction

"A Strategy for Systems Implementation," David Tommela presents strategies for rapid attainment of systems benefits and for improved systems quality with minimal impact on users and reduced pressure on the DP department.

As part of their efforts to meet user demand for new systems, many DP installations have turned to packaged software. Finding, evaluating, and possibly modifying packaged software, however, is an often costly and risky process. Raymond P. Wenig, in "Selecting Software Packages," identifies the rewards and risks of using software packages and outlines the requisite steps for their successful acquisition.

For applications developed in-house, many DP managers rely on structured techniques to increase analyst/programmer productivity and user satisfaction. Pat Duran and Al McCready provide a general overview of these techniques, explain the reasons for using them, and outline their benefits in Chapter Eleven.

Whether software is developed in-house or acquired from a vendor, legal issues surround its ownership, use, and disclosure. In a chapter refreshingly free from legalese, Susan H. Nycum discusses the current legal status of software and the types of protection available; she also provides suggestions that can help users and developers of software obtain full legal protection.

Perhaps no other aspect of DP management has gained as much public attention in recent years as computer security. Well-publicized computer-related crimes, disasters, and breaches of privacy have all contributed to heightened public awareness of security and privacy issues and increased the pressure on DP managers to protect their organizations' information resources. In his chapter on computer security, Jagdish R. Dalal provides a general overview of security problems and outlines procedures for developing and maintaining a cost-effective security program.

1 DP Management: A Modern Challenge

by Robert E. Umbaugh

INTRODUCTION

Twenty-five years ago, the first general-purpose business computing equipment entered the market. With it came opportunities for significant improvements in productivity.

Initially, the most common application, in business and government, was accounting. It was not unusual, therefore, for the computing function to develop in the department of the controller. The equipment, in the form of the electronic accounting machine (EAM), frequently appeared before there were enough people qualified to wire and run it. As applications began to extend beyond accounts receivable and payable, the job of EAM room supervisor often fell to the individual most adept at plug board manipulation. He or she had no formal supervisory training—but simply developed along with the job.

Just as the early aircraft leaders were those pilots who survived the experiments and crashes of the first planes, the first EAM room supervisors were those who survived the early failures of DP experimentation. Very often, these imaginative pioneers saw beyond the most obvious first steps in applying this new technology to the business environment.

As the value of the EAM was proven and its applicability transcended the bounds of accounting, new problems arose. For the first time, the self-trained EAM supervisor had to deal with multiple users and the resulting need to allocate resources. Priorities had to be established, user requirements had to be more formally documented, and supervisors had to become familiar with such new functions as inventory control. These demands placed new burdens on the EAM supervisors, some of whom were now being called DP managers. Significantly, DP budgets were now beginning to catch the attention of top management. Although some new managers were able to handle these complex demands, many were not.

THE MEANING OF DP MANAGEMENT

What were the factors that caused so many managers to fail? The answer lies in the nature of the job as it evolved. Data processing technology has progressed at extraordinary rates. From primitive beginnings, it has become one of the central functions in the modern organizational structure, whether in business, academia, or government. Most organizations now depend on the reliable and continuing operation of a computer. Relatively few executives, however, understand the workings of a computer; in fact, most are in awe of it. The DP manager, then, must bear the responsibility for properly applying this technology to the problems of the organization.

The DP manager has become "the man in the middle," although he is often unprepared for the task. This is a tremendous responsibility and one that many have unwittingly assumed. It is unreasonable to assume that a person can automatically progress from supervisor to manager. A supervisor deals with short-range objectives, a limited mixture of resources, and a limited number of tasks. He or she is usually not concerned with long-range trade-offs or resource acquisition. Supervisor contacts are usually with people at a similar corporate position. Opportunities to investigate the intricacy of the total organization are, therefore, rare. This did not pose a problem when the demands on the DP manager or supervisor were relatively simple and contained; however, this is not the case today.

Information that required a month of processing 25 years ago can now be processed in a matter of minutes. The modern DP staff often numbers in the hundreds; applications are huge, interrelated, time dependent, and critical to the continued operation of an enterprise. Compare the task of processing accounts payable 25 years ago with providing real-time support for a manned lunar landing. This evolution has extended to distributed DP, which enables computer technology to affect virtually every facet of society. As the cost of DP hardware continues to decrease and as the number and variety of applications increases, the demands placed on the DP manager will become more intense.

THE MODERN DP MANAGER

Just a few years ago, DP managers could handle their jobs adequately if they could successfully interact with other middle managers, guide the installation of moderate-sized applications systems, and run a batch operation. Because of the complexity of current applications systems and top management's increasing awareness of data processing, DP managers must now acquire a broad range of managerial and technical skills. They must also consider skills that may be required to qualify them for further advancement.

Certain trends suggest the type of specialized education, varied experience, and managerial ability that are essential to the DP manager's basic job repertoire.

The DP Manager's Environment

The methods of increasing and measuring the productivity of an entire organization will become much more important in the near future. As U.S. industries begin to approach the reasonable limits of profitable return on investment that accrue from substitution of machinery for blue collar labor and increasing skilled and professional labor costs, management will turn its attention to improving the productivity of clerical and white collar labor. The application of computer technology in productivity improvement will be an obvious choice. We have seen preliminary indications of this in WP and office automation. Word processing is in the first stages of evolution; however, its effective use on a broad basis will require the techniques, discipline, and skills already employed in data processing.

Methods of measuring productivity will also become a DP task. This measurement will be concerned less with work than with the products, services, and goals of the total organization.

Another trend is the increasing limitation of funds available for "discretionary" investment. DP managers find themselves competing for funds with other members of the enterprise; this competition will probably become more intense as the cost of capital (interest) continues to be high.

A third trend is the increasing complexity of the business and governmental environments. Addressing of outside issues now occupies a major part of top management's time, and this is more likely to increase than decrease in the future. Top management will have to delegate more responsibility and authority to lower levels of the organization, and this will undoubtedly change the nature of daily operations.

Further evidence of a rapidly changing environment can be found in the advances of DP technology. Between 1972 and 1979, the cost of processing one million instructions was reduced by 44 percent, the cost of storing data on direct access devices decreased by 70 percent, the cost of a CRT was reduced by 40 percent, and the cost of mainframe memory decreased by an astonishing 97 percent. In contrast to the decreases in hardware costs during this time, the price of assembly-line machinery increased by 80 percent, the cost of raw materials increased by 120 percent, and construction costs rose by more than 60 percent. It is projected that the cost of labor will increase by 120 percent during the 1980s, but output per man-hour will rise only 15 percent.

While the lower price of hardware makes it an attractive means of increasing work force productivity, the complexities resulting from the many configurations available to the buyer pose another problem for the DP manager. The DP manager must make many choices: mainframe size (how about plug compatibles?); memory size (how about a buffer?); and number of channels, front ends, disks, drums, tapes, mass storage, terminals, modems, line speeds, printers, and so on. After considering configuration options, the DP manager has to deal with acquisition options: direct purchase, monthly rental, third-party leasing, or the possibility of acquiring used equipment. The DP manager must consider methods of system usage: time sharing, service bureaus, or in-house processing. Decisions must then be made on contract negotiations and the many approaches to applications development. Additional problems are posed by personnel and funding: staff, training, budgets, job priorities, and security. In order to deal with these challenges, the DP manager needs extensive exposure to several disciplines.

JOB SKILLS OF THE DP MANAGER

In a survey [1] recently conducted among West Coast executives who had formerly been DP managers, Fred Held found the following set of characteristics:

- Knowledge of the total organization—a comprehensive understanding of organizational operations, objectives, problems, personnel, and management philosophy
- Line and staff experience—a demonstrated ability to manage a line function and to perform in a high-level staff position
- Ability to deal with complex issues—experience with EEO/Affirmative Action, privacy of data, business ethics, Occupational Safety and Health Administration standards, union requirements, modification of mandatory retirement policies, environmental concerns, consumerism, and other issues
- Multiple-site experience—working experience with a multilocation or multinational company and an understanding of the communications and logistics problems of a multisite enterprise
- Planning experience—operating experience in developing and executing short-, mid-, and long-range plans; the ability to integrate DP plans with all other functions of the enterprise; and experience in dealing with top management during the planning process
- Large-scale budget experience—ability to assign priorities to proposed projects, allocate discretionary funds, and understand budgeting concepts
- Project management experience—ability to conform to predefined budget, schedule, and end-product specifications
- Middle-management experience—demonstrated experience as a productive and cooperative member of a middle-management team
- Technological experience—demonstrated ability in dealing with a high-technology organization and in directing the resources of that technology to solve problems to benefit the organization as a whole

To this list can be added personnel development experience, which can be defined as demonstrated ability in developing subordinates and in training a DP manager replacement.

The Importance of Education

The importance of formal education in the DP profession has been debated for years. It is obvious, however, that the environment in which a DP manager must operate is quite complex. In order to prepare for competition in this environment, the DP manager must be exposed to two formal bodies of knowledge: technology and business.

Technical education is a matter of keeping up with general technology without especially trying to learn all details of hardware and software. This technical education may be organized around installed equipment, even to the extent of being site specific. The DP manager should relegate the bits and bytes to subordinates and concentrate on becoming familiar with the general aspects of DP technology and managerial techniques.

As for managerial education, some people advocate an MBA for all who aspire to executive ranks. While there is a certain value in the knowledge and discipline gained while working toward the degree, it is not, by itself, critical for success. The modern DP manager requires the training provided by courses in finance, business law, governmental regulation, time management, human relations, business modeling, and business ethics. If one were available, a course on survival in corporate politics would be indispensable for an aspiring DP manager.

Programs containing most of these subjects are available as "executive programs" at many colleges and universities. They are generally four- to eight-week, full-time, live-in study programs where participants meet managers from other organizations as well as faculty. These programs are generally of high quality and are usually expensive. It is the DP manager's responsibility to seek out such a program and convince management that the investment would be worthwhile.

The Value of Experience

Obtaining the varied experience with and exposure to all components of an organization cannot happen by accident. This aspect of the DP manager's executive development likewise requires planning and commitment.

While it may be impracticable to expect to gain actual working experience in all areas of an enterprise, it is possible to become generally acquainted with them. The most common method used by the executives Held surveyed was participation in corporate-level committees or task forces. Being appointed a member of such a committee may require nothing more than an expression of interest. If your organization has an executive committee or similar body, initiate your effort by attending committee meetings that deal with subjects of interest. Another valuable source of corporate information is the formal organizational plan, if one exists.

Cross-training is usually difficult to arrange for DP managers because of the limited number of people who can assume their jobs while they are on assignment in other departments or divisions. This fact should not, however, dissuade DP managers from attempting to arrange such cross-training.

All too frequently, there are reports of DP shops that are not coordinated with their parent organizations—shops that are building application systems that are of greater technical interest than of real value to the enterprise. Such DP tactics indicate an absence of perspective on top management needs. In order to avoid this, the DP manager must look for opportunities to become involved in corporate-level planning and decision making. Without this important information, the DP department will only be able to react to, rather than anticipate and participate in, corporate development.

COMMUNICATING WITH TOP MANAGEMENT

How often have these words been heard: "Top management doesn't understand me," or "We've got to get top management to understand data processing"? The problem is not getting top management to understand DP but rather getting DP to understand top management. The successful DP manager must recognize that he is competing for scarce corporate resources in the form of money and staff and, scarcest of all resources, for top management time and attention. It may come as a shock to some DP managers that DP is not the most important function in all organizations. Data processing is a support function and, as such, exists only to support corporate goals and objectives. If it cannot do this, it does not have a right to exist. Data processing is valued by top management only to the extent that it successfully executes a support role.

Improving communication with top management, although an important area of responsibility for a DP manager, is difficult to discuss in general terms because personalities differ greatly from one organization to another. The management style of the total organization is directly related to the style of top management itself. Few top managers want to be directly involved in the management of data processing. All too frequently, the rare contact between the DP manager and the top executive occurs when the former approaches the latter for a significant budget increase in order to acquire another large computer. These sessions usually have decidedly negative overtones. The DP manager must be able to meet top management on a positive basis. This requires careful planning so that such meetings do not appear contrived.

There are, in fact, methods of using these meetings to benefit both parties. Since such opportunities occur only occasionally, the DP manager should make every effort to ensure that his goals are accomplished. He should know in advance what he wants to achieve from the meeting and precisely what he wants to discuss during the session. His presentation should be succinct, businesslike, and terminated clearly and promptly. Most important of all, the DP manager should not oversell. Top-level managers did not achieve their positions by being naive. Those who hold these top positions can usually spot a phony very quickly. The DP manager will be accepted by and considered a member of top management much more quickly if he is able to accept top management's point of view on the allocation of resources.

In communicating with top management, the DP manager should avoid using technical terms and jargon, as they only widen the chasm between the two parties. The DP manager should learn to present data processing in terms of return on investment. Present-value analysis should be used when assessing proposed projects; the direct financial impact of such projects on organizational objectives should be stressed. Less time should be spent on justifying the newest piece of computer hardware and more on assessing the long-term contributions that DP can make to corporate goals.

Written progress reports to top management are excellent tools for the DP manager to use to demonstrate his understanding of the total enterprise. Written reports should be concise and should include progress against predetermined schedules, budgets, and objectives. Objectives should include a narrative of goals, the names of individuals responsible, and the dates by which projects should be completed.

Care should be taken to set realistic objectives. Projections should not be made until specifications for the individual product are known. Just as a builder would not give a cost estimate for a multistoried office building until he knew the proposed size of the building, its location, and its mix of materials, the DP manager should not be tempted to give "ball park" figures for a major new system until he knows fairly precisely what the system is expected to do, how often it will be run, and whom it will serve. General estimates tend to become set objectives, causing inevitable cost and schedule overruns, and succeed only in further reducing the credibility of the entire DP department.

Style. While on the subject, a few suggestions can be made about the importance of creating a good appearance before top management. First and foremost, remember that top management greatly values time. Be well organized. A DP manager who stumbles through a presentation, shuffling slides or flip charts and handing out reams of exhibits filled with charts, tables, and acronyms, cannot expect to achieve his purpose.

Do not discuss more than one or two major topics during any one session. Be precise. Tell management what you want, why you want it, and how it helps the enterprise; ask for approval; then conclude the presentation. Be as organized in your departure as in your arrival. If, for instance, you use flip charts or large exhibits during your presentation, leave them in the conference room and then retrieve them after everyone has gone.

If there is one single element that is most influential in separating those who succeed in climbing into executive ranks from those who do not, it is probably public speaking ability—the ability to make a good oral presentation before a group. If you are at all dissatisfied with your speaking skills, begin a program now to improve them. Accept speaking assignments in risk-free or low-risk situations so that when an important presentation comes along (as it will) you will be prepared for it. As a general observation, those who are most likely to succeed are well dressed, conservative in appearance, and self-confident. You should never permit your style of dress to detract from your message.

CONCLUSION

If we were to describe the successful DP manager, one who would be a likely candidate for advancement, he or she would, first, help to develop a corporate policy on data processing. That policy should contain, among other things, a statement of the organization's approach to DP and a concise description of the DP department, its responsibilities, and how its performance is measured. The manager should have a formal, written plan for DP, containing statements on applications development, staffing, training, hardware, software, facilities, security, and costs.

The successful DP manager will be properly prepared to direct and lead the implementation of this plan by acquiring both the experience and education needed. He will demonstrate perseverance in implementing the plan while, at the same time, recognizing that the environment in which he operates will change. He will have considered alternative courses of action and have established contingency plans where appropriate.

He will be flexible enough to overcome short-term failures in order to achieve more important long-range goals. He will be generally inquisitive, well-read, and capable of speaking intelligently on subjects other than the speed of his mainframe.

He will have carefully built and protected a reputation for getting things done through others and for being able to look beyond the confines of his own department in order to contribute to the growth of the organization. He will be an asset to the corporation, rather than a drain on its resources. He will abstain from playing corporate politics and will remember that a function such as DP operates in a fishbowl for all of the organization to see. Above all, he will conduct himself ethically and avoid procrastination, remembering that putting off until tomorrow what should be done today only guarantees no tomorrows.

Although promotion of the DP manager is not directly guaranteed by outstanding leadership of the DP department, it is certainly more likely to occur as a result of such success. In order to free himself for promotion, the DP manager must select and train a replacement. The person likely to be promoted from DP manager to a higher level must recognize that if guiding the department is difficult, the next step will probably be even more demanding. He must assure himself that he both wants and can handle the larger responsibility. The wise manager will not accept an appointment in which success is not probable. While the rewards of advancement are great, so, too, are the responsibilities. Not everyone is destined to captain the fleet.

Reference

1. Survey conducted by Fred Held, Vice President, Operations Planning and Purchasing, Mattel Toys, Hawthorne CA 90250. Permission to quote granted.

2 Long-Range Planning

by Louis Fried

INTRODUCTION

Despite more than 20 years of experience with computers, corporate and DP management still face unhappy surprises from their DP installations. These surprises frequently result from failures in long-range planning. Principles of strategic planning, which have been adopted by most major corporations, rely heavily on computer sciences; they have, for the most part, not been adopted by the computer managers themselves.

Excuses in support of short-range planning are numerous. They include frequent changes in hardware and software technology, rapid personnel turnover, constant changes in system requirements, and the frequency of unexpected user demands. These factors indicate the changing environment of which DP is a part. Many DP managers fail to realize, however, that they themselves are agents of change; consequently, they should help plan how those changes will occur.

A long-range plan for DP should include the following elements:
- Systems
- Hardware
- Software
- Staffing
- Control

THE SYSTEMS PLAN

Developing the systems plan is probably the most time-consuming and critical portion of any long-range planning effort. DP management must familiarize themselves with corporate and divisional plans, the organizational structure, business methods of the firm, and its product lines. They must develop a clear concept of how the various functions of the organization interrelate and how the systems currently operated by the DP department assist these functions. One method of establishing this picture is to prepare a flowchart of the business (see Figure 2-1). The chart can be enhanced by identifying the organizational responsibility of each function and identifying which functions are and are not computer supported.

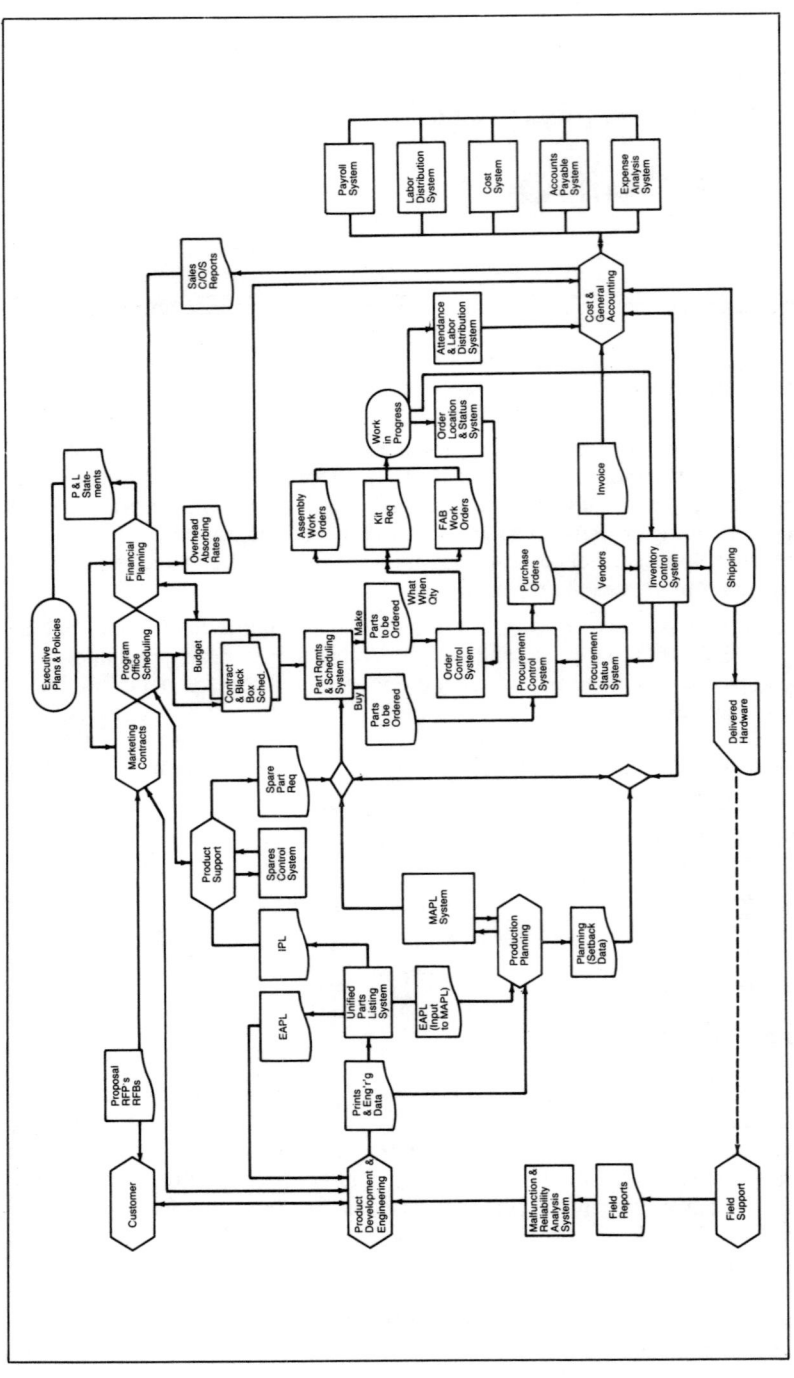

Figure 2-1. DP Planning: Business Flowchart

LONG-RANGE PLANNING 11

Each DP system should be reviewed and described in such a manner as to provide a basis for establishing other parts of the plan. These descriptions should contain the following information:

- A brief summary of the application, indicating pertinent features of the system and an idea of the stability of the system and future development plans. Each DP system should be reviewed with its users to determine areas of potential change or enhancement. If, as is frequently the case, users are not familiar enough with computer capabilities to assist in this planning, the planning staff may have to define potential changes and enhancements. These plans should then be reviewed with the users. This section should also indicate the input method and the record volumes of the most critical files. Volumes should be indicated for the current time period and projected for one, two, and five years.
- Equipment requirements for the system. Core requirements should be indicated in bytes or words and should represent the largest core-resident program segment of the system. Peripheral devices should be summarized and should represent the combined requirements of all programs in the system. It should be noted whether equipment requirements are for a central computer, a minicomputer operating in a distributed processing environment, an intelligent terminal, or a combination of these. This also applies to all other elements of the system description.
- File sizes stated in terms of characters and representing the greatest number of characters required online in the system at a single time.
- Computer hours stated in terms of schedule requirements; a daily figure representing the hours required during a 24-hour period; a weekly figure representing the hours required for those portions of the system scheduled to run on a weekly basis, and a monthly figure representing the time required to run jobs scheduled on a monthly basis. Computer time should be divided into activity shifts to permit later analysis of the need for multiprogramming scheduling.
- The number of programs written and the programming languages in which they are written, provided as an aid to estimating future hardware plans.
- Requirements for specialized systems software. Examples should include terminal control software, telecommunications, monitors, data base management systems, data dictionaries, report generators, and similar software. This information is especially significant when planning a distributed processing environment.
- Telecommunications equipment in use, described in terms of type of equipment, application, line configurations, network layouts, line speeds and loads, and so on.

Planning Systems Support

The planning group next must turn its attention to those areas that are not computer supported. System projections for those functions should be based on the following information:

- A review of potential changes of these functions with the responsible organization units
- An examination of the function for automation potential
- An outline of a systems concept (a brief flowchart and five or fewer pages of narrative)
- A review of the systems concept with potential users
- A final technical system concept paper
- A description of system resource requirements prepared in the same manner as for existing systems
- An estimate of the computer resources necessary for developing, testing, and converting the new applications

After documenting the potential changes for the existing systems and for anticipated systems, prepare cost estimates for development, implementation, and continuing operation. Considering the current cost of operating the function, current and future capacities of the systems, the systems' flexibility, and the economic effect on current labor-intensive methods, prepare a chart for each application, showing the projected cost of current versus proposed methods over five years. Using the same material, prepare a pay-back analysis for each application.

Isolate potential changes or new applications that do not appear economically feasible and that are amenable to noncomputer solutions.

The result is a descriptive list of financially feasible applications and solutions to problems that cannot be solved without the use of a computer. This document should be reviewed with management.

The selected applications should be examined for priority in terms of cash availability, return on investment, consistency with long-range corporate plans, and anticipated environmental conditions. This is a top-management task.

Experience indicates that the most productive approach to this task is to establish a DP steering committee. This committee should be established by the organization's president, who should also chair the committee, and should include the heads of all major user groups. The steering committee should be responsible for approving the long-range plan, approving individual segments of the plan, and monitoring DP performance. After the committee has established the priorities of the approved applications, the documentation of this data becomes the basic long-range systems plan.

THE HARDWARE PLAN

The information provided by the control reports, combined with projections of volumes for current systems and information on new systems from the systems plan, provides the basis for forecasting hardware needs.

The hardware plan should include the following items:
- Central computer (e.g., model, size, channels)
- Other computers (front ends, minicomputers, special-purpose equipment)

LONG-RANGE PLANNING 13

- Storage devices (e.g., DASD, tape, archival storage)
- Terminals (type, use, location)
- Communications (e.g., modems, multiplexors, lines)
- Data entry equipment
- Support equipment (e.g., decollators, tape cleaners)
- Facilities (e.g., space, power, air conditioning)
- Any other capital or rental equipment requirements

For these items, the plan should include a year-by-year statement of capacities, capabilities, locations, costs, and methods of transition from present configurations to future ones. Transition methods may require that reference be made to the staffing and software plans. In fact, in order to relate properly to each other, the hardware, software, and staffing plans should be developed concurrently.

The long-range plan has one principal feature that distinguishes it from a short-range plan—it is a projection of hardware, software, and cost trends.

Within limits, routine perusal of currently published materials will provide an adequate indication of general trends in hardware and software.

Another useful parameter is business economics. A computer manufacturer will want to obtain sufficient return on investment in a new product line before making it comparatively obsolete. It can be generally assumed that a computer product line will be replaced within eight to ten years by a new offering that has greater capacity and capability, for less money. A company should not plan to acquire a computer at or near the end of its life cycle without prior study and justification. Such justification is possible (e.g., purchasing a used computer near the end of its life cycle can provide substantial savings).

Given various software options and a staffing level consistent with the expense level authorized by top management, a schedule should be developed for implementing the applications on a priority basis. In addition to indicating manpower and software requirements, the schedule should indicate the time necessary for system development and operation. This schedule becomes the basis for the hardware plan.

Since the planned applications represent an extension or replacement of the current work load, a summary of the data shown on the descriptions of present applications must be integrated with the expected additional work load of planned applications and development work. This can be charted by showing a baseline for estimating average computer utilization, considering the net effect of replacement and showing the anticipated impact of future applications (see Figure 2-2). To be consistent, estimates should be made in terms of the performance of the current hardware. Total anticipated main memory and peripheral unit needs should be estimated on the basis of the needs of the systems that are currently, or are expected to be, operating concurrently in multiprogramming mode.

Having established these requirements, the next step is equipment evaluation. This phase should consider technical evaluation and possible benchmarking of equipment from various manufacturers, the single- or multiple-vendor situation, and the purchase versus lease or rent position.

DATA PROCESSING MANAGEMENT

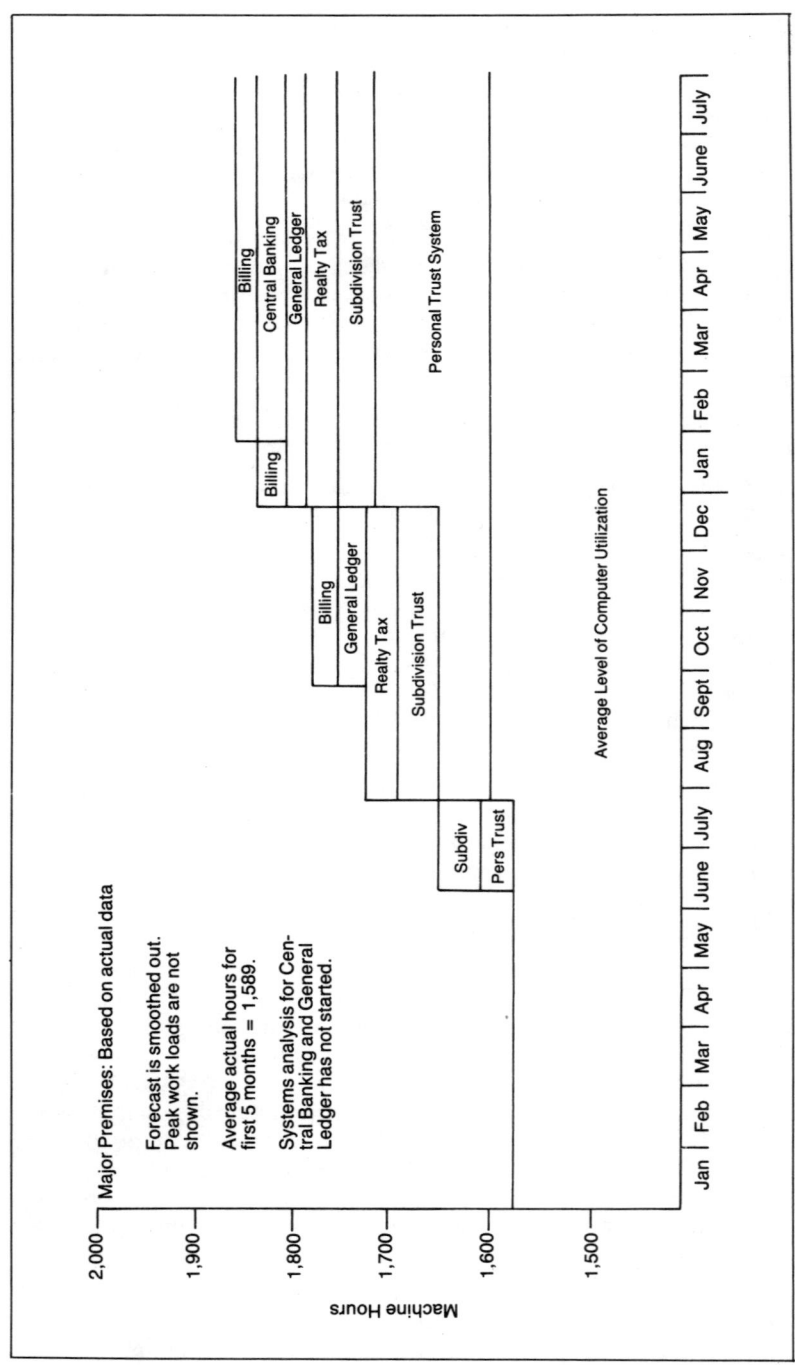

Figure 2-2. DP Planning: Estimated Average Computer Utilization

LONG-RANGE PLANNING

The purchase versus lease or rent decision should be based on the following factors:
- Present age of the product line being considered (or age of the product line at time of anticipated purchase)
- Estimated sale value of the equipment at time of next anticipated equipment change
- Cost of money
- Cash flow over the expected life of the installation
- Present value of future cash flow dollars
- Taxes and investment tax credits
- Depreciation schedule
- Lease termination penalties

THE SOFTWARE PLAN

The software plan, developed concurrently with the hardware and staffing plans, will influence and be influenced by both plans.

The characteristics of the operating system will influence hardware selection as well as the training and caliber of the staff required for the installation. Some operating systems require the purchase of several auxiliary packages. On the other hand, an efficient operating system can reduce hardware requirements.

In order to meet the objectives of the systems plan, conversion of the operating systems may be required. Such a conversion will have major impact on staffing and must be considered in the schedule of system implementation and hardware delivery.

Systems software must be selected according to application, development, and operating requirements. The following list is intended to suggest some of the considerations for systems software:
- Application requirements
  - Data communications monitor
  - Terminal control software
  - Data base management system
  - Inquiry system
  - Report generator
- Development requirements
  - All of the above
  - Data dictionary system
  - Program library management system
  - Program performance monitor
  - Online programming system
  - Debugging and documentation systems
- Operating requirements
  - Program library management system
  - Tape library system
  - Hardware monitor analysis reports
  - Computer-time-accounting system

A similar list must be drawn up for any minicomputers in a distributed environment and for any network control software.

Documentation and technical standards must be reviewed and plans developed for their maintenance and enhancement. A change of operating systems, for example, will require major changes in the standards of the installation.

The software plan creates additional budgetary needs caused by the anticipated price of software, the anticipated cost of conversions, and estimated amounts for upgrading and maintaining documentation and technical standards.

THE STAFFING PLAN

A staffing plan should project specifics for 18 months and show general projections for at least another 12 months. The result should be a chart (see Figure 2-3) and supporting documentation.

On the basis of the software systems selected, the staffing plan should designate the caliber and type of personnel required (development, clerical, or operations). Anticipated salaries should be based on the current market. It may be necessary to consider using outside consultants or temporary personnel for peak loads. A training program should be devised for the continued development of personnel resources.

The ability to meet staffing requirements will have an effect on the schedule of the hardware, software, and systems plans.

THE CONTROL PLAN

The control plan includes the policies, procedures, and techniques necessary to provide DP and general management with the tools necessary to control the direction and monitor the performance of the DP department.

Many of the elements of a good strategic plan, and a long-range plan, are based on the results of current management techniques and performance evaluation methods.

Management control depends on quality reporting that emphasizes performance evaluation and cost-effectiveness. Reports should:
- Evaluate by measuring actual performance against a predetermined standard
- Be oriented toward the function being measured
- Cover all functions
- Predict trends
- Enable management to anticipate potential problems or unusual expenses
- Be concise and readable and interpret—graphic in presentation, when possible
- Chart a 13-month period to indicate trends
- Support structural continuity from the lowest level of the organization to top management

LONG-RANGE PLANNING

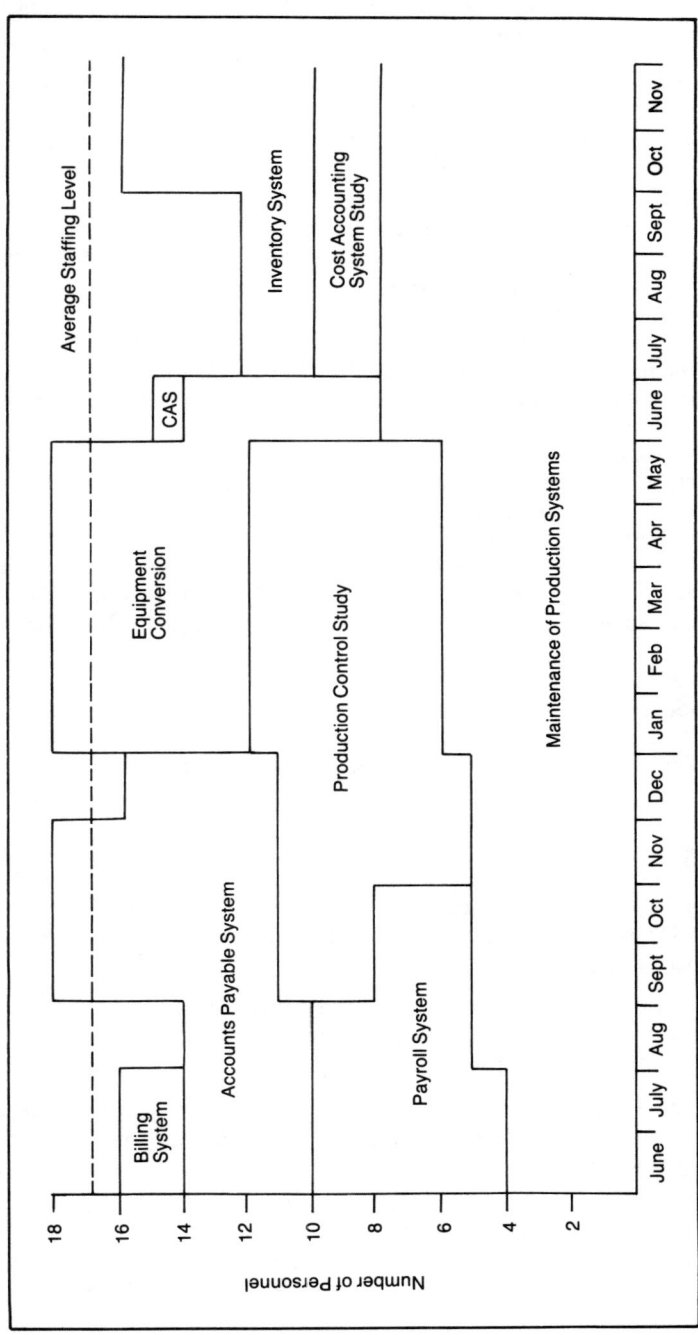

Figure 2-3. DP Planning: Staffing Requirements

- Be received by management routinely and promptly enough to permit timely corrective action

For example, the operations manager should receive the following types of reports:
- System downtime report—This report should track system downtime against performance targets, by reason (e.g., CPU, program, peripheral, air conditioning, or power failure, operator error).
- Rerun time report—This report should track rerun time chargeable to the data center, by reason. Rerun time is defined as the total time required to complete the job less the time used for the final, good run.
- User-caused rerun time report—This report should track machine time required as a result of user-caused reruns. This is useful in identifying problems in the system or in isolating training deficiencies. In a time-sharing environment, this report helps to trace and correct any repeated abuses of the system by terminal users.
- Peripheral performance report—This report should contain the frequency and duration of and reasons for downtime for each peripheral device. This helps to identify failure-prone units requiring service or replacement. This report should cover terminal devices.
- Data entry performance—This report should compare expected versus actual performance in keystrokes for the data entry group. (The data entry manager needs this information by individual to evaluate performance.)
- Data entry volume—This report should show budgeted versus actual work load in terms of input documents or records keyed by job.
- CPU performance reports—A series of reports should be developed to indicate capacity used versus capacity available in the CPU. Such reports should clearly separate the capacity used in the systems state from that used in the problem state.
- Computer utilization summary—This report should indicate available capacity and its use in productive time, downtime, and rerun time. Trends aid capacity planning.
- DASD capacity summary—This graphic report should track available capacity versus file space allocated.

Other reports that may prove useful include performance tracking of terminal response time, channel utilization, communications-line failures, on-time report distribution, and control errors.

These reports detect trouble spots requiring action and provide capacity utilization trends for long-term planning. They also indicate long-term potential staffing and training needs.

An essential tool for performance monitoring is a system for charging project development and operation costs to users. These charges should include overhead factors that result in the recovery of all DP costs by the DP organization. Guidelines must be established to control project cost and time on a regular basis.

LONG-RANGE PLANNING

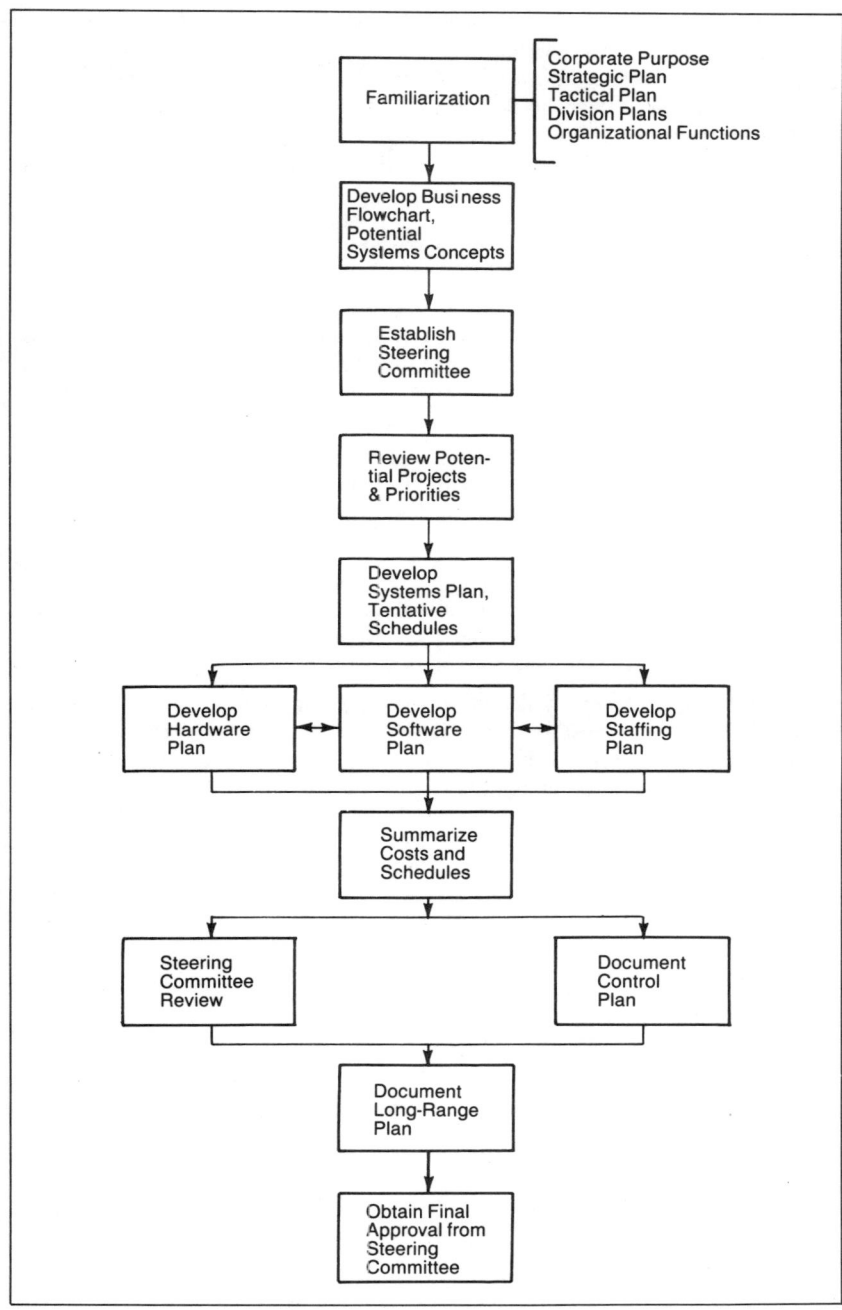

Figure 2-4. DP Planning: The Long-Range Plan

A steering committee should establish policies for the approval of new projects in a manner similar to approval for capital investment. During the life of a project, various checkpoints should be established at which the steering committee can make go/no-go decisions on continued investment in the project. The steering committee should also receive regular reports on project progress and should review project priorities every six months or as often as necessary to meet changing conditions.

MAINTAINING THE LONG-RANGE PLAN

Organizations new to long-range planning (see Figure 2-4) will find that their first long-range plan will take from six months to a year to develop. This means that, prior to publication, some of the information contained in the plan may be as much as a year old. A final prepublication review will be necessary to bring all information and projections up to date.

External conditions may have considerable impact on any long-range plan. For that reason, it is necessary to maintain continuous research and to report project progress regularly. At least every six months, a progress report to the steering committee should indicate accomplishments and deviations from the long-range plan.

The DP manager will benefit from the long-range plan by being able to prevent crises through a deeper understanding of the company's requirements and through a closer liaison with top management.

Corporate management will benefit from the plan by establishing control over the DP effort, increasing familiarity with the uses of information processing technology, and avoiding the high cost of crash programs and unanticipated equipment and software conversions.

③ DP Steering Committees

by the AUERBACH Editorial Staff

INTRODUCTION

An organization's DP function is somewhat like a company within a company. It is a highly complex, technically oriented function that has counterparts to all functions of a manufacturing concern (e.g., engineering, production, quality control). Data processing operates both a job shop and a continuous production shop, and it often provides services to all segments of the organization.

In many ways DP is an alien body within the host organization and, if not controlled, can cause serious damage to the host. There have been many instances of runaway DP costs caused by lack of control or executive "computer fever." In addition, the DP industry is replete with examples of failed projects, dissatisfied users, inappropriate priorities, lack of communication with users, high turnover, and other ills often linked with weak DP management. Because of these problems, DP sometimes requires control methods that would not be applied to any other internal function.

Some of the problems faced by DP managers result from an improper reporting level for DP, a lack of DP manager involvement in strategic planning for the organization, and less-than-perfect peer relations with other high-level managers in the corporate structure. Steering committees are usually established to address problems that arise from one or more of these factors and to ensure proper coordination between top-management objectives and DP plans.

THE APPROACH

A steering committee is an advisory group empowered to make top-level decisions for a function for which it is not directly responsible. The committee reports to the top echelon of the organization and is delegated specific executive powers. Each member of the steering committee is partially responsible for the effective use of the resource that the committee oversees.

Essentially, the steering committee operates as a board of directors. While not generally making detailed operating decisions, the committee establishes priorities, controls expenses, and makes economic and policy rulings. One difference between the DP steering committee and a board of directors is that a board usually contributes to the expansion of an organization, while the steering committee often works to limit and control DP expansion. When the decision is made to limit DP costs, the committee creates for itself the problems of allocating a limited and expensive resource and resolving the political problems arising from contention for this resource.

There are two types of DP steering committees. The permanent steering committee is responsible for the overall guidance of the DP function; the temporary or project steering committee is responsible for the successful completion of individual projects.

PERMANENT STEERING COMMITTEE

Because DP costs run as high as seven percent of the gross revenues of an organization, the permanent steering committee should include the president or chief operating officer of the organization and those executives whose departments use DP services. Regardless of the DP manager's reporting relationship, he or she should also be a member.

The duties of the permanent steering committee usually include the following:
- Use the members' knowledge of the organization's strategic and tactical plans to determine appropriate levels of DP expenditure and capability.
- Approve specific proposals for acquisition of major DP equipment.
- Approve long- and short-range DP plans.
- Determine whether specific projects are to be undertaken. These decisions are based on expected return on investments, lack of alternative methods, anticipated impact on the organization, and conformity with corporate long-range plans.
- Determine project priorities.
- Review and approve cost allocation methods.
- Review project progress.
- At specific decision points, determine whether projects should be continued or abandoned.
- Resolve territorial and political conflicts arising from the impact of new systems.

Because these duties require ongoing attention, the permanent steering committee should meet regularly—preferably on a monthly basis.

Advantages

The permanent steering committee can enhance the DP function by providing the benefits that follow.

Management Awareness. The steering committee can gradually educate management concerning the factors affecting the cost and efficiency of the DP function. During one steering committee meeting in which the annual DP budget was being discussed, the president of the company asked, "Why is

STEERING COMMITTEES

money allocated to program maintenance? Can't you get these programs right the first time? I don't see why you should have to touch a program unless a change is requested." The problems of program maintenance were explained to the president as clearly as possible, but he still did not seem convinced. Later, two charts (see Figures 3-1 and 3-2) were used as an aid in explaining the problems of systems design and programming. The impact on program performance and stability of changes in the operating system, the compiler, the hardware, and the user environment were also explained.

Manufacturing	Systems Implementation
Customer requirement established	Problem recognized
Customer specifications drawn and request for quotation released	Problem definition, system survey
Applications engineering study	System synthesis
Bid or quotation	System proposal
Product engineering	System specification
Manufacturing engineering	Program definition
Production	Programming, manual writing, etc.
Quality control	Systems testing
Prototype test or first article qualification	Parallel operation
Delivery	Implementation

Figure 3-1. Comparison between Systems Implementation and Manufacturing Functions

Manufacturing	Systems Implementation
Production standards available	Production standards often not applicable
Performance a factor of group average effort	Performance a factor of individual aptitude, background, and speed
Operations clearly defined	Operations require creative skills
Specifications known from customer	Specifications to be developed as part of project
Product to meet limited flexibility requirements	System to provide maximum flexibility
Limited coordination needed	Constant coordination and approval required

Figure 3-2. Dissimilarities between Systems Implementation and Manufacturing Functions

Thus, the permanent steering committee provides a forum for conveying concepts, while discussing specific issues or projects. These concepts should be conveyed in noncomputer language whenever possible.

DP Coordination with Long-Range Plans. Another benefit is that the steering committee can ensure the continued coordination of the DP function with the organization's long-range plans. The steering committee provides a vehicle for conveying organizational plans to the DP manager. In addition, it allows top management to apply its knowledge of the organization's plans directly to the management of the DP function.

Cost Control. While the DP manager is responsible for maintaining control of DP budgets and expenditures, the steering committee is responsible for monitoring expenditure levels and for correcting deficiencies in the control mechanisms used by the DP manager. Annually, the committee should review the DP budget, which should detail DP expenditures as well as their allocation to the user departments. This review allows committee members to determine how their operations will be affected by DP costs and provides an opportunity to explore alternatives that may reduce costs or permit more effective use of funds.

Establishing and Reviewing Priorities. The committee also establishes and reviews project priorities. Inappropriate priority setting is probably second only to project failure as a cause of high DP manager turnover. The steering committee has the broad knowledge and authority to assign effective project priorities. As an adjunct to this function, the committee can also approve additional resource acquisitions to meet commitments or to cancel or delay lower-priority projects if necessary. It is essential that the steering committee regularly review the priorities of all ongoing projects to prevent inappropriate allocation of the organization's resources.

Project Approval and Review. The steering committee also approves new projects and reviews projects in progress to evaluate their viability and to prevent overcommitment of resources without securing adequate return. A new project proposal should contain most of the elements illustrated in Figure 3-3. The detailed proposal is usually prepared by the DP group, but the DP manager should *not* present the proposal to the steering committee—this task should be performed by the member of the committee for whom the project will be done.

New System Proposal

1. A statement of the request and a description of the system
2. A statement of the need for the system
3. Analysis of the financial return on the system
    a. Discount rate for cash flow (five-year life suggested)
    b. Return on investment
    c. Pay-back period
    d. Gross annual savings (e.g., personnel, machine use)
    e. Annual costs (including depreciation and maintenance)
    f. Net savings
    g. Annual cash flow
4. Timing of the installation
5. Alternative approaches examined
6. A work plan or Pert chart for implementation and installation of the system
7. Plans for conversion from existing facilities and methods
8. Any supporting attachments or exhibits
9. Management approvals

Figure 3-3. Elements of a Project Proposal

STEERING COMMITTEES 25

Most steering committees require that projects exceeding a minimum dollar cost be submitted for approval (a figure of $40,000 may be appropriate). Any substantial change to the estimated cost of an approved project must be sanctioned by the committee. Monthly reporting of project status can provide the committee with an early warning system to stop potentially unproductive projects. The monthly report can be structured as illustrated in Figure 3-4.

Resolution of Internal Conflicts. The steering committee is responsible for resolving political and economic conflicts at the highest level. The committee meetings provide a forum for resolving such conflicts by group interaction or by presidential guidance, without making the DP manager the "man in the middle."

Executive-DP Manager Interaction. The steering committee continually educates the DP manager concerning the thought processes and operating methods of the top-level executives. Such interaction is a significant benefit for the DP manager. Of course, there is a corresponding risk involved: The DP

Status Report
January 1983

1. **Name of Project:** Employee Benefit Statements
2. **Project Leader:** Joyce Bowland
3. **Project Cost ($):** Period ending January 22, 1983

	Labor	Computer	Total
Current Month:	14,088	2,035	16,123
Project-to-Date:	27,715	4,100	31,815

4. **Estimated Cost to Complete:** 7,800   1,500   9,300
5. **Estimated Cost at Completion:** 35,500   5,600   41,100
6. **Original Estimated Cost:** 31,000   6,000   37,000

	Installation	Completion
7. Original Scheduled Completion Date:	1/31/1983	2/28/1983
8. Estimated Completion Date:	2/15/1983	2/28/1983

9. **Purpose:**
   The system will provide the capability to produce the annual Employee Benefits Statement ready for mailing during the first week of March every year. An annual $28,000 reduction in operating cost is anticipated.

10. **January Results:**
    By January 22, all programs were in the final stages of program testing. The various production runs necessary to create the year-end files were proceeding without problems.

11. **February Schedule:**
    Complete testing and verify all programs. If necessary, run special updates to payroll and retirement income files to correct data.

    Print Annual Benefits Statement.

    Complete documentation of the system and all procedures.

12. **Problems:**
    Turnaround time continues to be a problem.

Figure 3-4. Sample Monthly Project Status Report

manager is also exposed to the evaluation and judgment of executives. This exposure is only a danger for the incompetent, however; a well-prepared, effective DP manager should welcome it.

Disadvantages

Perhaps the most common problem with permanent steering committees is poor attendance. The people who should serve on the committee are the executives with the greatest number of pressing responsibilities. Three strategies can help improve attendance:
- The president of the organization should be chairman of the committee and should stress the importance of regular attendance. Without this support, the committee is likely to fail.
- Good staff work is required by the DP manager. Presentations should be precise, clear, pertinent, and should avoid DP jargon at all costs. Visual aids should be developed carefully and in a uniform format. Status reports and proposals for new projects should be distributed in advance.
- Meetings should be brief and businesslike. Top management appreciates subordinates who recognize the value of their time and who act accordingly.

There are other potential disadvantages associated with the steering committee approach. The major problems and recommended corrective actions are discussed in the sections that follow.

Uninformed Action. Occasionally, a steering committee acts precipitously and makes a decision or takes action that is counterproductive. This action can be very difficult to reverse, and the effect can be widespread. Good staff work, proper education, and occasional lobbying can help avoid this pitfall.

Squeaky Wheel Syndrome. This is a well-known malady, usually resulting in an inappropriate distribution of "grease." As with most cases of overlubrication, it usually causes a mess in the long-run. The solution is strong leadership on the part of the chairman. It is his or her responsibility to ensure that the actions taken are in the best interests of the whole organization rather than of a single individual or department.

Insulation. The committee may actually insulate the DP manager from top management if it is not properly structured or if alternates are permitted to sit in for the principal committee members. The purpose of the committee is to involve top management with the DP function rather than to insulate it. The solution to this problem is proper membership on the committee and stringent attendance requirements supported by the chairman.

The Stall. This problem is also called "analysis paralysis." Committees sometimes avoid difficult decisions by recommending further study. The solution to this common problem is to define a specific goal and a means for achieving it prior to entering the meeting. The member making a presentation should specify the decision or action desired and structure the presentation so that it leads logically to a conclusion or a specific recommendation.

The "Picky, Picky" Syndrome. In this syndrome the committee starts out with noble objectives, such as setting high-level priorities and approving major projects and equipment acquisitions; these objectives degrade progressively until the committee is bogged down with choosing modem vendors and interviewing applicants for computer operator positions. This may be helpful if the DP manager's goal is to keep the committee occupied with trivia while he or she runs the show; however, if effective upper management involvement in DP is the goal, then this problem must be avoided. This syndrome is more easily prevented than cured—the DP manager should ensure that the committee has a clearly established charter and should work with the chairman to help the committee follow the charter.

Total Usurpation. In this case the steering committee steers as well as designs, builds, modifies, maintains, and often wrecks the DP function by gradually assuming full management responsibility and turning the DP manager into a highly paid, highly frustrated clerk. The only corrective action is to work to abolish the committee and start over or to find another job.

An Alternative

If the organization already has an executive or management committee whose function is to provide overall policy and planning guidance to the organization, this group may be able to oversee the DP function. In this case, however, the committee's involvement must be limited to matters of major significance, such as setting overall priorities and establishing departmental spending limits. The DP manager must be an effective and decisive manager in order to work with this type of committee.

PROJECT STEERING COMMITTEE

As discussed previously, project steering committees can perform some useful functions at the project level. They can be used whether or not the organization has a permanent DP steering committee. The project steering committee is structured so that the chairman has direct management responsibility for the project's success. (The chairman is usually the executive in charge of the user group who initiated the request.) Committee members should include executives from other groups in the organization who may be affected by the system, managers of the user functions that will be involved with the system, the DP manager, and the DP project manager.

The functions of the project steering committee include:
- Review and approve the schedule for project tasks and segments. Segments of the project should be constructed so that the decision to continue the project can be made at several checkpoints.

- Monitor project progress by reviewing periodic reports from the development team.
- Ensure that the resources required for successful completion of the project are available.
- Resolve territorial conflicts among users and among members of the development team.
- Make major systems design and budgetary decisions.
- Provide management direction to the DP project manager.

The success of the project steering committee depends mainly on the clear understanding that the chairman is directly responsible to corporate management for successful completion of the project.

The project steering committee provides a major benefit for the DP manager. By giving the user total responsibility for the successful implementation of the system, it restricts the responsibility of the DP manager to the proper area—providing the required DP support functions.

The user also receives benefits. Steering committee reviews provide greater assurance that the system design specifications meet his or her requirements, that adequate acceptance testing is performed, that the proper resources are available at the right time, and that a workable conversion schedule is planned. In addition, the costs of the project are more visible, allowing more effective control of project expenses.

CONCLUSION

The DP steering committee can be a useful tool for organizations experiencing problems in coordinating DP activities with corporate objectives. Before deciding to use a steering committee, however, top management should consider alternative solutions, such as changing the reporting relationships of the DP function. If a steering committee is created, the DP manager will need all of his or her managerial skills to work effectively with it. The guidelines that have been presented can help the organization avoid the problems that plague many steering committees and ensure that the committee performs the function for which it was created.

4 DP Policies and Procedures

by Robert E. Umbaugh

INTRODUCTION

Policies, procedures, methods, directives, standards—known by different names and found in varying levels of detail, these written guidelines are necessary for the successful direction of any medium- to large-scale organization. They enable management to convey its wishes to large numbers of subordinates over a long period of time. Some managers mistakenly assume that directives contained in various memos, supplemented by effective and frequent oral communication, provide sufficient guidance for the organization. Such communication is essential; however, while the spoken word is occasionally more effective, the written word endures.

The following sections:
- Describe the elements of an effective procedures manual
- Instruct the DP manager on developing a manual
- Describe how to improve an existing manual
- Suggest sample formats
- Suggest roles for various individuals in developing a manual or series of manuals
- Provide a handy checklist for developing and maintaining a procedures manual

THE DIFFERENCE BETWEEN POLICIES AND PROCEDURES

Policies perform the following functions:
- Facilitate the exercise of executive leadership
- Establish authorized guidelines to achieve consistency in decision making
- Allow greater delegation of decision making to lower levels of management
- Communicate the principles and rules that will guide management decisions and employee action

Policies are the *what* of executive management; they state the philosophy and strategy of that group and provide an umbrella for all other written guidelines.

APPENDIX A shows a sample corporate-level policy statement for data processing.

Procedures, on the other hand, describe *how* to implement corporate and departmental policies. They are generally much more detailed than policy statements, often providing step-by-step instructions for specific tasks. They should indicate specifically when, where, why, and by whom tasks should be done. In this chapter, the term "procedures manual" is used generically and includes manuals on such subjects as standards and operating instructions.

COORDINATION WITH CORPORATE POLICIES

It must be remembered that DP policies and procedures cannot be developed in a vacuum; they must not conflict with other existing corporate policies and procedures. Where DP policies touch on issues covered by general corporate policies, a reference to the appropriate section in the general corporate policy statement should be included. If it is inconvenient for DP personnel to check the corporate policy statement in such situations, it may be a good idea to include the pertinent passage in the DP policies (together with a cross-reference).

Most large organizations have groups responsible for the preparation of corporate-level policies and procedures. While such groups are often of little assistance in developing standards manuals and other technical guidelines for DP, they can be helpful in the preparation of corporate-level policies for DP as well as generalized procedures. At the very least, it is important that the DP manager and others involved in preparing DP procedures coordinate their activities with the corporate-level group, if one exists.

ADMINISTERING PROCEDURES

Administering a procedures manual can be a full-time job in a very large DP installation. Responsibility for the development and maintenance of procedures manuals should be assigned to one individual, and that person should be accountable for meeting development schedules. This person should also be responsible for setting format requirements for procedures and for providing editorial assistance to those actually writing the procedures.

Since no single person is knowledgeable enough to write every procedure needed in a large DP installation, it is helpful to assign each procedure to a sponsor. The sponsor should be the person most knowledgeable about the subject (not necessarily the manager of that particular function). Management's role in the development of a procedures manual is no different from its role in other DP functions; management should give direction and review and approve the finished product but should not assume responsibility for developing the details of each procedure.

Updating Procedures

Once the procedures manual is written, it must be kept up to date. An obsolete procedure is sometimes worse than no procedure at all because some

POLICIES AND PROCEDURES 31

people will religiously follow written directives, no matter how outdated. The IBM ATMS or a similar text management and retrieval system can facilitate the updating process. For installations without such a system, WP equipment can aid in performing updates.

Some installations have found it helpful to schedule a regular review date for all procedures (e.g., every 18 months). Regular reviews help ensure that all existing procedures are timely and pertinent. If a procedure is not cancelled or drastically rewritten occasionally, the review process is probably not working effectively.

Indexing Procedures

An index must be developed for the procedures manual. A good index will save DP personnel time in using the manual and provide a handy tool for the DP manager, who can use it as a checklist during development of the manual, as a tool for ensuring that procedures are reviewed for timeliness and applicability, and as a quick reference for verifying that current issues, regulations, rules, and so on are included in the manual.

If the installation uses a keyword software tool, a keyword index can be used. Such an index is very useful; eventually, more than one procedure will address the same subject from different perspectives, and a keyword index helps to ensure consistency.

INTERPRETING POLICIES AND PROCEDURES

One responsibility often overlooked during the development of a procedures manual is interpretation. Since it is difficult to write every policy and procedure so that only one interpretation is possible, the subject of interpretation should be addressed before conflict arises. One approach is to assign responsibility for interpretation to the appropriate functional manager (i.e., procedures dealing with computer operations are interpreted by the operations manager, and so on). Another approach is to give the sponsor responsibility for interpretation. A word of caution is appropriate here, however, since the interpretation of policies and procedures involves some measure of authority, and the DP manager may not think it wise to grant this authority to the writer of the procedure. The safest course may be for the DP manager to reserve the right of interpretation. In practice, interpretation is seldom necessary; however, the DP manager should decide how to handle the problem should it develop.

INTRODUCING PROCEDURES

Introducing formalized procedures into an organization that has no or few written procedures can be compared with introducing a computerized system into a manually operated user department. The normal work routine will be disrupted somewhat, and orientation and training will be needed. Some employees will welcome the improved control process, and some will be uncomfortable or even hostile about the formalized procedures.

To minimize such problems, the process of developing and implementing a DP procedures manual should follow all of the steps used in the development of a computerized system:
- Analysis of the "problem"
- Prioritization
- Development
- Implementation phase
- Testing for inconsistencies and omissions
- Maintenance

The introduction of a formalized procedures manual requires discipline and should not be attempted on an ad hoc basis. It should be considered a formal project with all the appropriate attendant controls.

Orienting Employees

The author has found that it is wise to review each procedure with affected employees as the procedures are developed. The manager involved should give the employees an opportunity to read the procedures and then should cover the highlights and conduct a question and answer period. This may seem a considerable effort; however, managers should not assume that employees have read and understood and will follow written directions. Here again, an analogy can be drawn to the installation of a new computerized system: proper orientation and training are essential for success.

New Employees

It is especially important that new employees be given a complete orientation to departmental procedures and those corporate policies and procedures that are likely to affect them. A new employee handbook especially designed for DP employees is a good idea. (If the organization already has a handbook for new employees, a supplement for DP employees will suffice.) This handbook can be used as the textbook for orientation classes, introduce new employees to installation practices, and help them settle in their new work environment. A well-designed new-employee handbook can boost the productivity of newcomers, who will become productive much faster if they can avoid fumbling with housekeeping chores and searching for applicable standards. (A more detailed discussion of the handbook appears later in this chapter.)

PROCEDURES AND ORGANIZATIONAL STRUCTURE

As mentioned previously, policies and procedures should reflect and support the organization's management style. Tightly controlled installations are more likely to develop comprehensive and detailed procedures manuals, while organizations in which subordinate managers have more autonomy may develop fewer procedures.

Policies and Procedures in a Distributed Environment

A decentralized or distributed environment presents special problems when developing policies and procedures. A procedures manual for a decentralized or distributed system should contain the same basic elements as a manual for a centralized environment; however, the unique requirements of the decentralized environment must be taken into consideration. For example, maintaining physical and data security is more difficult in a decentralized environment, and security standards should be emphasized to ensure that the risk of exposure is minimized.

A decentralized operation is less likely to have the same quality of management available to all employees, and the probability of loss of continuity caused by turnover is much greater. In addition, the relatively smaller staffs at local sites usually have less specialized technical talent. These factors necessitate more detailed standards and procedures.

These same factors often lead to inadequate system documentation. If the organization is determined to maintain standard conventions, stringent documentation standards must be installed and enforced. If the organization wants to develop and maintain integrated systems in a distributed environment, measures necessary to integrate data and applications must be addressed in the procedures manual. Different naming conventions can make data and applications incompatible and make integration almost impossible.

Developing standards and procedures in a decentralized or distributed environment can be a problem in itself. If DP is totally decentralized and no central control group exists, it is unlikely that common standards and procedures can be developed. If a central control group does exist, however, this group should be responsible for developing standards. Individual procedures can be written by the various distributed sites; however, responsibility for controlling and reviewing the procedures should be centralized.

DEVELOPING A PROCEDURES MANUAL

For the DP manager who lacks a formal procedures manual but has many scattered formal and informal standards, gaining control of the operation may seem a formidable task. A structured process for formalizing procedures is the key to success.

The first step is to recognize that the installation needs improvement in the procedures area. The author has audited DP departments in which the absence of formal standards and procedures was a major cause of the installation's problems. Taking time to write down things may seem foolhardy when a shop is operating in a "disaster mode"; however, instituting formalized procedures can be of great help in gaining control.

Once the need for procedures has been acknowledged, the DP manager should resolve to develop them—immediately. Postponing the task will only aggravate the situation.

INVOLVING SUPERVISORS AND EMPLOYEES

While the DP manager may be the first to recognize the need for better overall control of the department, first-line supervisors, project leaders, and other employees often have a better understanding of specific needs. The DP manager should use these personnel as a resource, asking them to identify all subjects for which procedures are needed. This is the first step in gaining their support for a formal procedures manual. The list developed from their recommendations will contain duplications and omissions; however, such a list provides a good starting point for the development process.

The DP manager should particularly heed input from supervisors. They receive pressure from subordinates, management, and users and are the key to implementing and enforcing the procedures that are developed. If your organization has existing procedures, supervisors can often identify those that are outdated or incomplete and recommend corrections.

One way to start a formalized procedures process is to have the supervisors prepare a project plan. They can also help identify one individual who will be responsible for implementing the project.

HELP FROM OTHERS

In most organizations significant improvement in procedures is possible. Many large DP installations have a formal set of standards covering the technical side of the operation (i.e., systems development, programming, and, in most cases, operations); however, many installations have not formalized procedures for other parts of the DP function. Often, many installation procedures are outdated; in some cases the distribution of the procedures to the employees is inadequate. Better organization of the procedures manual can increase its use throughout the organization and improve the productivity of the individuals using it.

Vendors are another source of ideas for improving a procedures manual. Quite often, they have documentation from other installations that can be made available to customers, and some vendors will provide documentation from their own installations. Professional organizations and other companies in similar industries can also be valuable sources of information on procedures and standards.

In addition, managers should not overlook the possibility of finding help within their own organizations. Frequently, large companies have procedures writing staffs that can help prepare procedures, provide editorial services for refining drafts, and help ensure that the format of the DP procedures is consistent with other corporate procedures.

PROCEDURES REVIEW BOARD

Using a review board during the development of formalized procedures can provide input from several disciplines, ensure appropriate levels of review and approval, and facilitate acceptance of procedures and standards. The function of the review board is to critically assess the appropriateness and thoroughness of written procedures before they are formally adopted. The review board is not a steering committee—it does not direct the project, and the project development team does not report to the review board. The board need not meet formally during the review process unless there is disagreement among board members concerning the acceptability of a procedure. It is recommended that procedures not be adopted unless unanimously accepted by the review board.

Review Board Members

If an organization has an internal EDP auditing group, the manager of this group should sit on the review board, along with senior members of DP management and, where appropriate, representatives of major user departments. Including users on the review board can help them understand the important role procedures and standards play in the system development process. In organizations that assign users to project teams, it is appropriate that users also have a chance to review the standards that will guide project development.

PROCEDURES DEVELOPMENT CONTROL

The development of a procedures manual should be formalized as a project and subjected to the types of project controls used on other DP projects of similar size. The procedures to be developed should be categorized and assigned priorities. A schedule should be developed, and regular progress reports should be submitted to DP management.

Categorizing Procedures. Some DP installations find it convenient to categorize procedures by organizational segment (i.e., systems and programming, central site computer operations, data entry, distributed operations). Other organizations find it more convenient to categorize procedures by function (i.e., systems development process, security and contingency planning, production systems). The categories used should depend on organizational style and the personal preference of management.

Assigning Priorities. The procedures to be written in developing a new manual or updating an existing one should be assigned priorities, with the highest priority given to procedures that have the greatest potential positive impact on the organization. Assigning priorities can be the responsibility of the ad hoc supervisory group that initiates the project or of the review board, if one is established.

Implementation Schedules. DP management should pay particular attention to the implementation schedule for the procedures manual. The schedule should be ambitious; however, it must reflect the fact that time will be required for procedures review by both DP management and the review board, before implementation.

Distribution. Once the procedures manual is developed, the problem of appropriate distribution must be addressed. A quick survey of the DP installation will probably identify some employees who have procedures or standards manuals they no longer need and some who require ready access to manuals they do not have. Many organizations have a central group controlling the distribution of procedures manuals to all departments. In such organizations the DP manager should work through this group.

GUIDELINES FOR PROCEDURES MANUALS

As with most project development efforts, creating a procedures manual is easier if the development team does not have to work from scratch, without models or guidelines based on previous efforts. This section includes practical tools and examples to help the DP manager to develop a procedures manual. The series of appendixes are intended to provide ideas and to stimulate thinking and are not rigid rules to be followed step by step. The appendixes include a sample procedures manual table of contents, a procedures development control sheet, a complete sample procedure illustrating the general format, and a table of contents for a new employee handbook.

When developing a procedures manual, it is important to ensure that the procedures will facilitate the operation and management of the DP department and not interfere with day-to-day functions. The procedures must not be so cumbersome that they reduce productivity; it is possible to impose so heavy an administrative burden on the technical staff that form takes precedence over substance.

Table of Contents

APPENDIX C is a comprehensive sample table of contents for a procedures manual. It is divided into three parts for convenience. This table is only an example and not an ideal list; such an exhaustive list of procedures may be inappropriate for a smaller installation. On the other hand, it may not be broad enough for a very large, highly complex installation. For an installation that is subject to stringent security requirements, a complete security manual could replace the scattered individual procedures on data security, physical security, and so on. A numbering system facilitating location of specific procedures and cross-referencing should be used.

General Format

APPENDIX D illustrates the general format for a procedure. The format may vary, depending on the type of procedure; however, the basic structure is the same. The sample procedure, included in its entirety, concerns time-sharing facilities.

This procedure is fairly simple and short; however, it contains all elements of a generalized procedure. It describes what services are available, how to go about obtaining them, who should be contacted for the various services, and how to use the services according to DP department guidelines. All acronyms are defined the first time they are used—a very helpful practice for people who understand only English.

Many procedures are longer and more complex than this one; however, a procedure should always cover only one subject.

Control Sheet

APPENDIX E is a sample control sheet that can be used when developing a procedures manual and to coordinate the maintenance schedule for all manuals. The control sheet lists the major sections of the manual, the individual responsible for completion or review, and the scheduled completion or review date. In this case, the control sheet is used as a review schedule. For example, the schedule indicates that primary responsibility for the procedure concerning distribution of DP reports is assigned to the computer operations manager. It also shows that this procedure is scheduled for review each August. If a procedures review board is used, a copy of this schedule should be distributed to all members of the board to inform them of the review dates for procedures under their control.

New Employee Handbook

As previously mentioned, APPENDIX F is a table of contents for a new employee handbook. With high turnover in the DP field and the resulting need to quickly and efficiently integrate new employees into the organization, it is very important to ensure that new employees have ready access to the information that they need to do their jobs. A manual especially prepared for new employees has proved useful at many installations.

This manual covers items that are useful for a new employee but that are less important as the employee becomes acclimated to the organization; thus, it is unnecessary to update copies of the manual once they are issued. It is necessary, however, to review the master copy of the manual periodically to ensure the timeliness of manuals currently being issued. The contents of such a manual can differ greatly, depending on an installation's customs, location, orientation procedures for new employees, and the degree to which other procedures can be used to integrate new employees. APPENDIX F lists the contents of a new employee handbook that has been in use for several years.

APPENDIX A

Sample Corporate DP Policy Statement

PRINCIPLE

The Company provides data processing equipment and services to meet operational, contractual, legal, or managerial requirements.

ACTION RULES

1. Data Processing Services
   A. Data processing services shall be provided to meet organizational needs, when approved and authorized by user and data processing management. Such services include:
      1. Systems analysis and program development
      2. System maintenance, including minor system design changes, upgrading of programs and/or documentation, requests for one-time reports or processing, procedure revisions, and report distribution changes
      3. In-house computer equipment or, in emergencies, outside equipment
      4. Computer processing by the batch processing method (either in an open- or closed-shop environment) and by a time-sharing method
   B. Requests for data processing services shall be submitted on an authorization form to the system sponsor, when designated, for approval and subsequent forwarding to data processing. Assessment of the technical and economic feasibility and determination of priorities between systems is the responsibility of data processing. Review of the functional and economic feasibility and determination of priorities within a major system is the responsibility of the system sponsor or requester.
   C. The manager of data processing shall recommend company-wide systems priorities to the management committee. Such priorities shall be communicated through the distribution of the data processing master plan. The department manager shall prioritize all requests originated within his/her organization.
   D. The use of time sharing shall be limited to computer applications that require interaction between the user and the computer on a real-time basis. Time-sharing services shall not be used to provide rapid turnaround for computer applications that can be served by another process at a lesser cost.
   E. Time sharing shall be performed on company-operated computers in preference to supplier-provided services when internal services (equipment and skilled personnel) and supporting computer programs are available.
   F. When company resources are unavailable or when proprietary programs, unique services, or other features are required, supplier-provided services shall be considered.
2. Supplier or Contract Services
   A. In addition to the normal prequalification of suppliers provided by the materials services department, suppliers and contract services must be approved as technically qualified by data processing prior to authorizing services.
   B. Discussions with outside suppliers to establish new services or renew existing services or to acquire programs (including acquisition of application program packages) shall be coordinated through the data processing technical support group or, for time-sharing services, through the engineering programming and processing department.

POLICIES AND PROCEDURES 39

3. Budgeting
    A. Data processing shall budget manpower, contract, and other associated costs for in-house systems development and maintenance and for computer processing costs for administrative systems.
    B. The user organization shall budget and control computer usage for open-shop processing and time-sharing services (both company and supplier provided) and shall assign accounting distribution for allocation of costs. User departments shall be charged for open-shop utilization of computer systems and for time-sharing processes at a rate approximating the cost of the equipment and supplies used.
    C. User organizations shall budget all supplier and contracted services, including software development and equipment costs, user manpower devoted to the development of open-shop engineering programs, and other manpower not specifically included in A and B.
4. Standards
    Standards for systems development, programming, languages, and hardware configurations shall be established by data processing to provide system compatibility among users and suppliers.
5. Exceptions
    Any deviations from the provisions set forth in this statement shall require the approval of the responsible user vice president and the manager of data processing.

DEFINITIONS

Batch processing: a method in which input to a given program, set of programs, or system is grouped before processing

Closed-shop operation: processing systems under the control and scheduling direction of data processing

Open-shop operation: processing of applications based on user demand, as resources allow, and generally not controlled in terms of validity of input and output by data processing

Time sharing: a method in which online interaction occurs between the user at a remote terminal and a central computer

APPENDIX B

Examples of Procedures

The following three examples are taken from actual procedures. In some cases only part of a procedure is included. The purpose of these samples is to give managers an idea of the level of detail that procedures should include.

LANGUAGE STANDARDS AND GUIDELINES

COBOL
(excerpt)

A. · Introduction
   The purpose of these standards and guidelines is to encourage a uniform style of COBOL programming that will:
   - Improve readability
   - Reduce program test time

- Provide programs that are easy to expand, modify, and maintain

These COBOL standards and guidelines are organized according to the divisions required to code a COBOL program. All statements preceded by (S) are mandatory standards. Other statements not so designated are guidelines. Additional techniques for improving efficiency can be obtained from:
- *IBM OS/VS COBOL Compiler and Library Programmer's Guide* (discusses programming, machine considerations, using the sort/merge feature, and fields of the global table)
- Formal training courses
- Technical support department

All COBOL users should have a copy of the *IBM VS COBOL for OS/VS* and *IBM OS/VS COBOL Compiler and Library Programmer's Guide* manuals.

B. General Considerations

(S): Programs are to be compiled under standard LANGLVL (2).

Spacing the Source Module Listing—The EJECT, SKIP1, SKIP2, and SKIP3 statements, when used properly, improve the readability of the source module.

Comments should be used when the information conveyed is essential to the reader.

C. Identification Division

(S): Program names (PROGRAM-ID) should conform to the standard program naming conventions (see the Program Naming Convention Procedure).

(S): The DATE-COMPILED option must be used. The current date will be inserted in its entirety during compilation.

(S): The DATE-WRITTEN option specifying month and year must be used.

The REMARKS area should briefly describe the program's purpose, input/output sources and destinations, general structure, and special problems and should identify all called modules and their purpose, all switches and their function, and all report numbers. A change log should identify production changes.

JOB SUBMISSION

Submitting Batch Jobs from RJE Facilities

A. General

A dial-up RJE (remote job entry) terminal is located in the engineering programming work space.

The terminal is a DATA 100 Model 76 consisting of a 600-card-per-minute card reader; a 1,250-line-per-minute, 132-column line printer; a CRT (cathode ray tube) operator station; a keyboard; a communications switch; and communications equipment.

The terminal can be linked to the IBM System/3033 computer system operating with special communications equipment. By throwing a communications-line switch, the RJE terminal can be connected to a Pacific Telephone 4,800-bit-per-second modem that will permit dialing and point-to-point communications linkup with various off-site computer centers. By loading the specific control program for the computer center, the communications link is completed, and processing can take place. The standard control programs now available support:
- IBM 360/20—in-house, 19.2K bits per second; off-site, 4,800 bits per second
- SPERRY UNIVAC 1108—4,800 bits per second
- CDC 200 User Terminal—4,800 bits per second
- CDC HASP User Terminal—4,800 bits per second

POLICIES AND PROCEDURES 41

The dial-up RJE terminal has been cost-justified to communicate with various off-site computer centers. Organizations requiring off-site processing can use the terminal during other than normal working hours and will be expected to pay some portion of the equipment cost, depending on the extent of use.

Because of the limited speeds of the equipment, large input and output jobs will be restricted according to a notice posted at the RJE site.

Assistance and/or training related to the operation of the equipment is provided by the engineering programming department.

B. RJE Support

Contact engineering programming personnel for specific information concerning the RJE operation.

DATA PROCESSING ADMINISTRATIVE SERVICES

Billing and Adjusting Charges for Computer Usage
(excerpt)

A. General
  1. User organizations budget for and assign accounting distribution for their use of data processing's computer systems for open-shop batch processing and time-sharing services. (See Corporate Policy Statement: *Data Processing Services*.)
  2. User organizations are charged for these services (chargeback) at rates approximating the cost of the equipment and supplies used.
  3. Chargeback (based on computer operation data) is billed monthly on the computer-prepared report *Computer Chargeback to User Departments* (see sections B and C, following).
  4. Data processing administrative services prepares and processes the accounting vouchers necessary to set up the charges (see section B, following).
  5. If certain conditions adversely affect the usefulness of the computer output, chargeback credits may be applied following investigation of requests from user organizations (see sections D and E, following).
B. Processing—Computer Chargeback to User Departments
  1. Computer preparation of the monthly chargeback report is usually completed by the fourth work day preceding the end of the month.
  2. Engineering programming receives a complete copy of the chargeback report for use in controlling its time-sharing and open-shop batch processing and plotting services for user departments other than data processing. This copy is used in handling inquiries by user organizations, including requests for chargeback adjustments. Engineering programming also receives a copy of the report on microfilm.
  3. Data processing administrative services receives a copy of the chargeback report and initially uses it to prepare the following vouchers:
     a. Chargeback: A monthly form 8-3-A (*Miscellaneous Journal Entries*) is prepared, charging the specified accounts of other (user) departments and crediting data processing's account 1023, *Computer Services Chargeback—Credit*. Account 1023 is used to offset expenses for computer equipment and related supplies in data processing accounts 1021 and 1022.
        (Note: Charges for outside services that are input to the system producing the chargeback report are excluded from form 8-3-A because they are charged directly to the user's account on payment.)
     b. Budget Control: A monthly form 8-4-A (*Transfer Voucher*) is prepared to

capture data for each of two methods of monitoring and controlling projects and systems.

(l) Expense Projects: Expense data is entered into this separate system by a charge to account 1021, *Computer Processing Equipment* (identified by a 4-digit expense project number), offset by a credit to account 1021 (no project number). Credit adjustments are entered by reversing the above debits and credits.

DATA PROCESSING ADMINISTRATIVE SERVICES

Billable Services and Rates

The rates and services shown here have been established for billing purposes. Examples for use of these rates are shown in procedure number 41, *Billing and Adjusting Charges for Computer Usage.*

Rates shown for batch, TSO, and mass storage charges are for System/3033 jobs submitted in any job class established in the category of normal processing. Deferred processing is also available at 50 percent of normal processing rates.

See procedure number 42.19 for specific job class assignment within each of the processing categories.

- Batch Charges
  - CPU Time: $0.08/second
  - Disk I/O: $0.30/1,000 accesses
  - Disk Mount: $2.00 each step
  - Tape I/O: $0.20/1,000 accesses
  - Tape Mount: $1.00 each step
  - Card Reader: $2.00/1,000 cards
  - Card Punch: $6.00/1,000 cards
  - Printer: $0.40/1,000 lines
- Time-Sharing Charges
  - CPU Time: $0.20/second
  - Disk I/O: $0.30/1,000 accesses
  - Connect Time: $1.00/hour
- Mass Storage Charges
  - Resident Disk Space: $0.15/track
  - Tape Rental: $1.00/month
    Note: One track on a 3350 can contain 190 card images of 80 characters each with a block size of 800 characters (blocking factor 10).
- Miscellaneous Charges
  - Microfilm: $0.10/1,000 lines
  - Plotting: $0.30/minute
  - Terminals, modems, phone lines: various charges
    Note: Contact network control center (NCC) of DP technical support for information on terminal charges/rates.

APPENDIX C

Procedures Manual Table of Contents

PART I—GENERAL DP PROCEDURES

Section 1. Policy
    Statement of Policy for Data Processing—DP Services   01.01.01

POLICIES AND PROCEDURES 43

      Provided
      Statement of the Jurisdiction of the Data Processing Department   01.01.02
      High-Level Organization Chart   01.01.03

Section 2. Procedures Relating to DP Administration
      Services Provided by Departmental Administration   01.02.01
      DP Budgeting Guidelines   01.02.02
      DP Training   01.02.03
      Tracking and Resolving DP Problems   01.02.04
      DP Service Goals   01.02.05
      Billable Services and Rates Charged   01.02.06
      Control and Payment of Supplier-Provided Time-Sharing Services   01.02.07
      Ordering DP Technical Publications   01.02.08

Section 3. Procedures Relating to Required DP Operating Documentation
      DP Operational Test Procedures   01.03.01
      Flowcharts   01.03.02
      Run Sheets   01.03.03
      SYSOUT Messages and Action to be Taken   01.03.04
      Production Restart Instructions   01.03.05
      External Tape Labels   01.03.06
      Distribution of DP Reports   01.03.07
      Off-Site Storage of Backup Data Sets   01.03.08
      Plotter Use Instructions   01.03.09
      Production Rerun Instructions   01.03.10
      Production Systems Trouble Call List   01.03.11

Section 4. Procedures Relating to Control and Balancing
      Detailed Procedures for Control and Balancing of Each Production Job (as appropriate)   01.04.01
      •
      •
      •

Section 5. Procedures Relating to Hardware Configuration and Capabilities
      Hardware Planning and Budgeting Guidelines   01.05.01
      Hardware Acquisition Process and Authorization Required   01.05.02
      Central System Configuration   01.05.03
      Distributed System Configuration—Approved Devices   01.05.04
      Data Network Configuration and Standards   01.05.05
      Plotter Description, Capability, Limitations   01.05.06
      Data Entry Device Configuration   01.05.07
      Scanner Device Configuration, Capability, Limitations   01.05.08
      Computer Output Microfilm Capability   01.05.09
      Report Distribution Equipment Configuration   01.05.10
      Time-Sharing Capabilities, Use, Authorizations   01.05.11
      Remote Job Entry   01.05.12

Section 6. Procedures Relating to Data Entry Standards and Guidelines
      Data Entry Standards—Source-Document Design Requirements   01.06.01

Submitting Work to Data Entry 01.06.02
Validation Requirements 01.06.03

Section 7. Procedures Relating to Job Submission
Submitting Batch Jobs from the DP Center 01.07.01
Submitting Batch Jobs from RJE Facilities 01.07.02
Submitting Jobs via TSO 01.07.03
Jobs Requesting Use of Microfiche 01.07.04
Jobs Requesting Use of Plotter 01.07.05

Section 8. Procedures Relating to Tapes and Tape Drive Management
Guidelines for Tape Use 01.08.01
The Tape Management System 01.08.02
Open-Shop Use of Closed-Shop Tape Data Sets 01.08.03

Section 9. Procedures Relating to Disk Space Management
Disk Data Set Classification and Guidelines 01.09.01
Data Set Archiving 01.09.02
Data Set Management 01.09.03
IMS Data Base Space Monitoring 01.09.04

Section 10. Procedures Relating to Job Control Language (JCL)
Preparation and Use of JOB Statement 01.10.01
Preparation and Use of EXEC Statement 01.10.02
Preparation and Use of DD Statement 01.10.03
Preparation and Use of the Job Entry Subsystem (JES) Control Statement 01.10.04
Preparation and Use of the INTERNAL READER 01.10.05
Job Classes 01.10.06
SYSOUT Classes 01.10.07
Job Entry Subsystem (JES) Form Numbers 01.10.08
Forms Control Buffer (FCB) Numbers 01.10.09

Section 11. Procedures Relating to Language Standards and Guidelines
COBOL 01.11.01
FORTRAN 01.11.02
PL/1 01.11.03
VS BASIC 01.11.04
Assembly Language 01.11.05

•
•
•

Section 12. Procedures Relating to S/370 Libraries
System Library Descriptions 01.12.01
Updating Production Libraries 01.12.02
Project Development Libraries 01.12.03

•
•
•

POLICIES AND PROCEDURES

Section 13. Procedures Relating to Naming Standards
    System/Subsystem Names   01.13.01
    PROC Names   01.13.02
    JOB Names   01.13.03
    Program Names   01.13.04
    Data Set Names   01.13.05
    Data Element Names   01.13.06
    Record Names   01.13.07
    IMS Naming Conventions   01.13.08
-
-
-

Section 14. Procedures Relating to Miscellaneous Services
    Programming Procedures Used with the Plotter   01.14.01
    IBM 3800 Plotting Facility   01.14.02
    Guidelines for the Use of Microfilm   01.14.03
    Use of the Form Slide   01.14.04
    Guidelines for the Use of an Optical Scanner   01.14.05
    Use of the IBM 3800 Printer   01.14.06

Section 15. Time-Sharing Services
    Time-Sharing Services Available   01.15.01
    Time-Sharing Facilities   01.15.02
    Programming Language Libraries   01.15.03
    Available Software Functions   01.15.04
    TSO Equipment   01.15.05
    Creating Your Own TSO Commands/CLISTS   01.15.06
    Special Commands   01.15.07
    Application Programs   01.15.08
    LOGON Procedures   01.15.09
    TSO Security   01.15.10
    TSO Data Set Accessing Conventions   01.15.11
    Creating and Modifying Data and Programs   01.15.12
    Nondisk Data for TSO Use   01.15.13
    Extended Commands Capability   01.15.14
    TSO/Batch Interface   01.15.15
    Data Set Conflicts   01.15.16
    Error Messages   01.15.17

Section 16. Procedures Relating to Non-DP Use of Computing Services
    Engineering Programming Services   01.16.01
    Computer Services Purchased from Outside   01.16.02
        Suppliers—Administration and Processing
    Engineering Application Computer Program   01.16.03
        Products—Acquisition and Installation
    Listing and Punching Card Decks   01.16.04

Section 17. Procedures Relating to the Data Dictionary/Directory
    Keywording   01.17.01
    Specialized Facilities Under DD/D   01.17.02

Section 18. Procedures Relating to UTILITIES and SUBPROGRAMS
    Detailed Procedures for Each UTILITY and SUBPROGRAM   01.18.01
    Available (as appropriate)
-
-
-

Section 19. Procedures Relating to Debugging and Tuning Aids
    Tuning Application Programs   01.19.01
    Detailed Procedures for Each Debugging Aid Available (as appropriate)   01.19.02
-
-
-

Section 20. Procedures Relating to Description of DP Systems
    This section should contain abstracts of each production system of major importance to the installation.   01.20.01
-
-
-

PART II—SYSTEMS DEVELOPMENT

Section 1. Procedures Relating to Project Management
    DP Project Management   02.01.01
    Project Staffing   02.01.02
    Project Schedules   02.01.03
    Project Status and Progress Reports—Overview   02.01.04
    Project Budgeting Guidelines   02.01.05
    Systems Development Standards Enforcement and Deviation   02.01.06
    Change Control Boards and Systems Advisory Committees   02.01.07

Section 2. Procedures Relating to Systems Development Cycle
    Systems Development Life Cycle—General Definition and Flow   02.02.01
    User Responsibilities   02.02.02
    Auditor Participation and Responsibilities   02.02.03
    Project Initiation   02.02.04
    General Specifications   02.02.05
    Detailed Design Specifications   02.02.06
    Ancillary Systems Design and Interface   02.02.07
    Standards and Guidelines for Forms Design   02.02.08

Section 3. Systems Design Specifications
    Standards and Guidelines for Phased Plans   02.03.01
    Preliminary Systems Design   02.03.02
    User Requirements Summary   02.03.03
    Major Project Change Control Procedures   02.03.04
    Training Plans   02.03.05
    Systems Design Acceptance Criteria   02.03.06
    Cost/Benefit Analysis and Reports Required   02.03.07

POLICIES AND PROCEDURES   47

Section 4. Procedures Relating to Structured Methods
    Detailed Procedures for Structured Processes Used (if appropriate)   02.04.01
-
-
-

Section 5. Procedures Relating to System Installation and Evaluation
    Systems Installation   02.05.01
    Operations Acceptance Criteria   02.05.02
    Installation Follow-Up—Problem Resolution   02.05.03
    Post-Implementation Audit Activities and Reports Required   02.05.04

Section 6. Procedures Relating to Project Reports
    Project Initiation Report—Standards and Guidelines   02.06.01
    General and Detailed Design Phase Reports—Standards and Guidelines   02.06.02
    Implementation Report—Standards and Guidelines   02.06.03
    Progress Reports—Contents and Standards—Distribution   02.06.04

Section 7. Procedures Relating to Systems Development Documentation Requirements
    General Requirements   02.07.01
    Indexing, Numbering, and Keywording   02.07.02
    Flowchart Symbols   02.07.03
    Transaction Flow Definition   02.07.04
    Data Requirements Definition   02.07.05
    Source Input Definition   02.07.06
    File Documentation   02.07.07
    Program Documentation   02.07.08
    Module Definition and Documentation   02.07.09
    Supporting Narrative   02.07.10
    Supporting Charts   02.07.11
    Benefits Matrix   02.07.12
    Central Systems Library Documentation Requirements   02.07.13
    Off-Site Storage of System Documentation   02.07.14
    Auditors Review of System Documentation   02.07.15

PART III—GENERAL ADMINISTRATIVE PROCEDURES

Section 1. Procedures Relating to Personnel Matters
    Manpower Budgeting, Recruiting, Testing, and Interviewing   03.01.01
    Processing Employee Expense Reports   03.01.02
    Maintenance of DP Personnel Records   03.01.03
    Involuntary Termination of Employment   03.01.04
    Employee Disciplinary Action   03.01.05
    Requests for Wage and Salary Action   03.01.06
    Premium (Overtime) Authorization   03.01.07
    Employee Training   03.01.08
    Processing New Employees   03.01.09
    Control of Absenteeism   03.01.10

Section 2. Procedures Relating to Procurement Activities
    Signature Authorization Levels   03.02.01
    Selection and Acquisition of DP Software—General   03.02.02
    Selection and Acquisition of DP Hardware—General   03.02.03
    Use of Outside Services for Appropriate Software Analysis and Programming   03.02.04
    Proprietary Software—Use and Safeguarding   03.02.05

Section 3. Procedures Relating to Security
    Pre-Employment Checks   03.03.01
    Admission to DP Centers   03.03.02
    Building Security/Emergency Procedures   03.03.03
    Physical Security Program Audit   03.03.04
    Contingency Planning   03.03.05
    Data Security   03.03.06

APPENDIX D

Sample Procedure Format

Procedure   01.15.02

TIME-SHARING SERVICES

Time-Sharing Facilities

Before you become a company time-sharing user, you should become familiar with the administrative controls and procedures as well as the technical facilities (both hardware and software) available to you. These aspects are discussed in the following sections:
    A. Time-Sharing Support Group (TSS)
    B. Time-Sharing Option (TSO) Program Development
    C. Time-Sharing Coordinator (TSC)
    D. Time-Sharing Terminal Acquisition
    E. User IDs, Passwords, Accounts, LOGON Procedures

A. Time-Sharing Support Service (TSS)

The time-sharing support service is staffed by members of the engineering programming section of data processing. Their function is to provide global support for all in-house and commercial time sharing at the company. TSS provides programming assistance, time-sharing problem resolution, and so on. They should be able to satisfy your technical needs with regard to time sharing at the company.

If at any time when using or attempting to use TSO, you experience hardware difficulties (e.g., if the computer does not answer the telephone), call the network control center (NCC) on 2-2329. TSO programming problems should be referred to TSS on 2-2968.

B. TSO Program Development

If you need to use TSO for an application for which you have no program, contact the TSS group. They will determine if the company has a program that can satisfy your

POLICIES AND PROCEDURES 49

request. If a program must be developed and the request is minor, no further action is required on your part. If the program requires a major effort, however, TSS will request that you submit a form 216 to justify the development of the program. Please reference procedure 01.15.01 for the necessary information to complete a form 216.

Occasionally, a program is cost-justified, but in-house development of the program is not. This may be the case, for example, if a program requires 100 man-hours to develop but will be used only once. In such situations, TSS will determine whether the program is available from a commercial time-sharing service. If it is, they will make arrangements to allow you to use the most cost-effective commercial service.

C. Time-Sharing Coordinator (TSC)

In order to provide a centralized source of information and control, each user department should have a time-sharing coordinator (TSC), selected by department management. The coordinators should control their department's use of both in-house and commercial time sharing. To obtain the name of a particular TSC, contact the TSS group. While technical questions about time sharing should normally be directed to the TSS group, administrative inquiries and problems should be directed to the TSC.

D. Time-Sharing Terminal Acquisition

The first thing you will need in order to use TSO is access to a terminal. To determine your department's terminal configuration and responsible TSC, please contact the TSS group. If your department does not have a terminal, the simplest means of acquiring access is to share with another department. The TSS group can assist in locating a terminal convenient to your working location and in providing the name of the TSC to be contacted. The TSC should know whether there is any available time on the terminal(s).

If there is no terminal available, or if you expect your use to be too great to be absorbed by existing equipment, you can request a terminal by completing a form 216. You should indicate the requirements for and the benefits to be derived from the installation of a new terminal. Approval depends on compliance with company policy regarding the use of data processing services. If the request is approved, the NCC selects the type of terminal and associated communication equipment that best suits the requirements of your particular application.

E. User IDs/Passwords/Account Number/LOGON Procedures

Access to TSO is secured through use of a user ID and password. Each user ID is a one- to seven-character password that identifies the user to the computer and is always kept secret in order to prevent unauthorized use of user IDs. Associated with this user ID is an account number that includes the account number or work order to which charges for your TSO sessions and disk storage are allocated. Also associated with this user ID is a LOGON procedure that is executed to initiate your TSO session and allocate required data sets.

Submit form 42-100 TSO (*User Identification Request*) to the data processing security administrator (DPSA) to obtain a user ID/password and establish an account number.

User IDs are assigned by data processing and are seldom changed. Passwords are initially assigned by data processing and are changed periodically by the user. It is your responsibility to maintain the confidentiality of your password. Every user has the ability to change his or her password at any time, with an allowable maximum of 89 days between password changes.

If an employee who has access to TSO terminates or transfers, it is the responsibility of the employee's supervisor to:
- Ensure that the password is changed
- Notify the DPSA by telephone of the actions taken

- Submit form 42-100 in order to delete the user ID or reestablish it as a valid user ID

The DPSA can be reached by calling the DP Trouble Desk (2-3600).

APPENDIX E

Data Processing Procedure Review Schedule

Review Codes:
M-Department Manager Q-DP Quality Assurance A-DP Administration
C-Computer Operations N-Data Network Operations D-Planning and Data Management
I-Information Systems O-Operating Systems Support E-Engineering Programming

Procedure No.	Subject	J	F	M	A	M	J	J	A	S	O	N	D
Section 1													
01.01.01	Data Processing Policy			M									
01.01.02	Data Processing Jurisdiction							M					
01.01.03	Organization Chart	A			A				A				
Section 3													
01.03.01	Operational Test Procedures				C								
01.03.02	Flowcharts							I					
01.03.03	Run Sheets											C	
01.03.04	SYSOUT Messages—Action	O											
01.03.05	Production Restart Instructions						Q						
01.03.06	External Tape Labels												O
01.03.07	Distribution of DP Reports										C		

APPENDIX F

New Employee Handbook Table of Contents

Section 1. Welcome to (Organization Name)
     DP Organization Chart (pictures are a nice touch)
     DP Jurisdiction Outline—Organizational Philosophy
     DP Policy Statement

Section 2. Plans and Objectives of Data Processing
     Formal Data Processing Plans
         Overview
         Where to Find Them

Section 3. Departmental Policies and Procedures
     DP Job Procedures
     DP Standards and Guidelines
     Request for DP Services—Form 216

POLICIES AND PROCEDURES 51

Section 4. Personnel Matters
    New Employee Status
    Employee Status Record—Personnel Files
    Employment Agreement—Security Agreement
    Performance Appraisals—Standards of Performance
    Career Development
    Employee Benefits—Overview
    Charitable Contributions—United Way
    Employee Savings Bond Program

Section 5. Office Hours, Timekeeping, and Pay Procedures
    Working Hours and Overtime
    Holidays
    Vacations
    Illness and Other Absences
    Timekeeping Records and Pay Procedures

Section 6. Security and Emergency Procedures
    Security Policies and Procedures
    Emergency Procedures
    Air Pollution Emergency Procedures

Section 7. Facilities and Services—DP Center and Corporate Headquarters
    DP and Corporate Headquarters Locations
    Entering the DP Center and Other Locations
    Supplies and Forms
    Reproduction Service
    Mail Services and Addressing Mail
    Telephone Services
    Transportation—Public, Car Pools
    Parking Information
    Banking Facilities and Automatic Payroll Deposit Service
    Medical Services and Pharmacy
    Central Systems Library and Other Libraries
    Typing and Clerical Services
    Conference Rooms—DP Center and Corporate Headquarters
    Employee Club Activities
    Tours of the DP Center
    DP Newsletter
    Suggestions and Questions
    Open Forums with Executives
    DP Training Room and Facilities

Section 8. New Employee Needs and Responsibilities for Certain Services and Products
    Supplying Operating Instructions for Computer Operations
    Designing Source Documents for Data Entry
    Obtaining Training in Use of Time-Sharing Option (TSO)
    Using and Preparing Corporate Procedures
    Understanding Basic Responsibilities of DP Technical Publications

Handling of Personnel Records and Office Facilities
Providing Corporate Open-Shop Time-Sharing User Support
Understanding Basic Responsibilities of Planning and Data Management Support of Application Systems
Responding to Matters Referred by the Problem Reporting and Tracking System
Relationships to Other Organizations Working in DP Center

Section 9. Data Processing Hardware and Software
Hardware and Data Communications Network
Software
IBM 370 Operating Status Signal Lights
Peripheral Equipment—Plotters, COM, Scanners

5 Management Control Reporting

by Louis Fried

INTRODUCTION

DP trends of the 1980s are extrapolations of the 1970s. Personnel costs are dominating DP budgets; hardware costs are decreasing; and the costs of communications, supplies, and incidentals are increasing. Computer system cost performance is improving at a rate of about 15 to 20 percent per year. The cost performance of communications is also improving but at a slower rate. As communications use increases, however, the cost for this service also goes up.

The cost of information systems accounts for an increasingly visible percentage of the gross revenue of most corporations. As a result, top management is demanding improved performance of the information systems function. One difficulty facing the director of the information systems function is providing management with appropriate tools for evaluating performance.

In many other areas of the company, performance evaluation is little more than measuring profitability or a return on investment. These measures, however, are usually not appropriate for the information systems function.

Yet, performance must be evaluated if top management intends to direct and control the activities of and benefit from the vital information systems function.

Performance control means managing for cost-effectiveness and benefits. In the past, many companies have established the policies governing information systems according to a philosophy of "minimizing the cost of information systems." More enlightened firms understand that if the information system's function is to properly contribute to corporate profitability, the philosophy underlying corporate information systems policy must "be to maximize the benefit from information systems cost-effectively."

Management based on this precept requires performance control over three areas:
- Operations
- Systems development and maintenance
- User interfaces with information systems

In operations, performance controls must apply to hardware, systems software, communications, service quality, and computer operation. In systems development and maintenance, controls must apply to projects and product quality. In the area of user interfaces, performance control can apply to response characteristics, such as request turnaround time, report production schedules, and terminal response time. In each preceding area, performance measures are applied to personnel as well.

PERFORMANCE CONTROL

Performance control depends on a feedback system that is oriented toward measuring and evaluating performance, resource utilization, and cost-effectiveness. In general, the purposes of management control are served by a feedback system that can measure both performance against a predetermined level of expectation and resource utilization against available capacity. Feedback system reports, capable of providing a comprehensive view of performance, should have the following characteristics:

- Reports should measure performance against a predetermined standard. Although most reports should preferably be quantitative, in certain circumstances only qualitative standards can be applied. For example, in measuring supervisory or management performance, a management by objectives (MBO) approach may be used.
- Reports should chart resource utilization against available capacity. This type of measurement can be used for computer hardware as well as for personnel and other resources.
- Reports must be oriented toward the function being measured, and the unit of measure must be appropriate and meaningful for that function.
- A comprehensive system should measure and evaluate all functions. Even those functions to which only qualitative measures can be applied should be controlled.
- A feedback system should assist the planning process by providing feedback reports that can be used to predict trends.
- In addition to predicting trends, reports should enable management to anticipate potential problems, such as increases in demand levels or unusual expenses.
- Reports should be concise and readable and should contain as little extraneous information as possible. Whenever possible, summary reports intended for higher managerial levels should be graphic.
- When quantitative measures are used, at least a 13-month period should be illustrated. This provides the historical perspective required for management control.
- The reporting structure should maintain continuity at every level of the organization. Repeated summarization should not destroy the audit trail or distort the information being presented.
- Feedback reports should be scheduled and delivered periodically (e.g., daily, weekly, monthly).
- Reports (e.g., cost justification and feasibility studies) should enable control of resource allocation and approval of major expenditures.
- The scheduling and delivery of feedback reports should be prompt enough to permit timely corrective action or changes in direction.

MANAGEMENT CONTROL REPORTING

Feedback system reporting supports a cooperative, coordinated management team within the information systems organization. If the reporting is honest, the feedback system can gain the support of top management by providing insight into the performance and needs of the information systems function and the ability to control that function through approval and priority-setting mechanisms.

REPORTING HIERARCHIES

Most organizations are structured in a scalar or hierarchic form that indicates delegation of authority and reporting relationships. Although these structures show lines of authority, they do not necessarily indicate information flow for control purposes. In fact, information flow is usually lateral, across organizational boundaries. In the routine course of business, such information flow is important to support decision making. With control information, this lateral information flow is essential because isolated organizations do not always have access to all performance indicators. Accommodating the lateral flow of information is a common corporate weakness.

Figure 5-1 is a classical organizational structure showing the place of operations in the overall management structure. This simplified form of organization can be used for comparison with the flow of information for operations control reports.

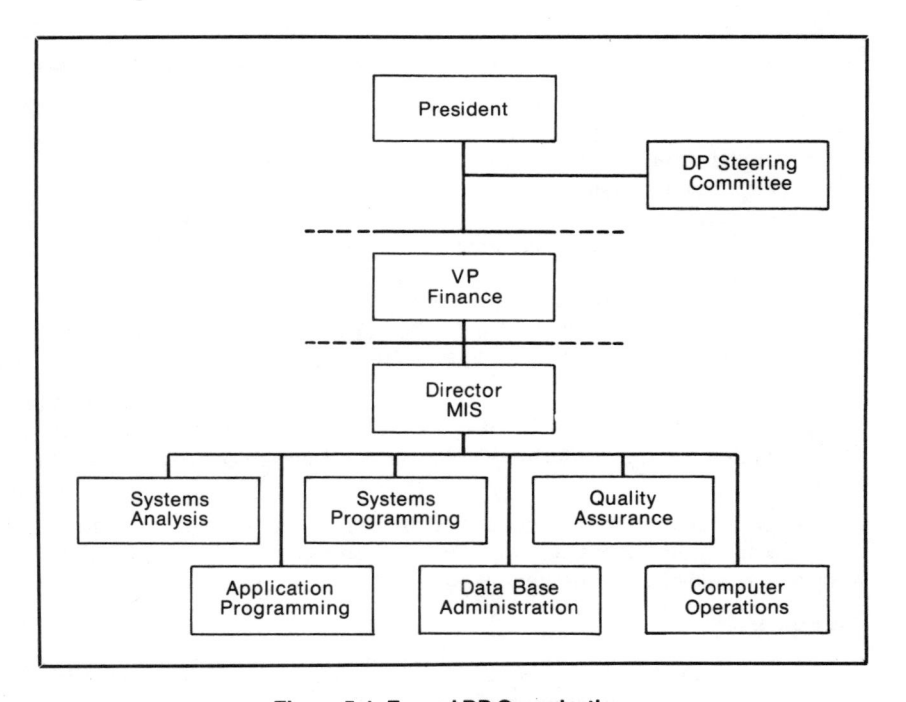

Figure 5-1. Formal DP Organization

Figure 5-2 shows that information is needed from areas outside of the control of the operations manager to provide that manager with a complete view of the organization. This information is summarized for upward communication to the director of MIS and may be further summarized for top management and the DP steering committee.

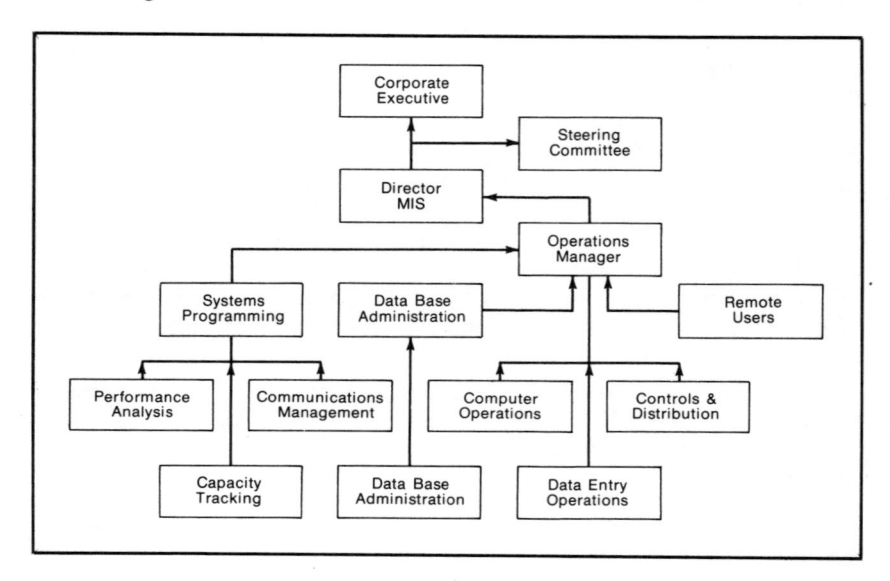

Figure 5-2. Operations Reporting Chain

Four organizational levels are concerned with information flow:
- Those who generate (or obtain) and validate the information
- Functional managers within the MIS area, such as the operations manager and others whose performance may be affected by the information gathered
- The manager of the DP function (e.g., the Director of MIS)
- Top management, which includes the corporate executive to whom the DP department reports as well as the DP steering committee

Information on performance moves up through this structure. The criteria against which performance is to be evaluated, however, are products of repeated iterations through the hierarchy, resulting in approval from the top down.

In a manner similar to the joint goal setting of an MBO program, performance criteria are ultimately a compromise of management desires, technical competence, and physical limitations.

METRICS

Metrics, the measures by which anything can be evaluated, are fairly straightforward for quantitative areas but are not accurate for qualitative areas.

MANAGEMENT CONTROL REPORTING

In either case, metrics must be selected and evaluation criteria established to support uniform, impartial, and consistent performance evaluation.

Quantitative measures can include:
- Transactions processed
- CPU cycles
- CPU time
- Lines printed
- Records keyed
- Reports delivered
- Terminal response time

Quantitative criteria applied to these measures can be based on known capacity limitations or management-determined performance standards. To aid in capacity planning and management, criteria are established by observing actual capacity (e.g., CPU time available by shifts worked, average hourly keystrokes for the entire data entry group, printer line-per-minute speed, online disk storage space available, and main memory available for application programs).

To aid in performance evaluation, criteria are based on standards. Examples of these standards include:
- A maximum five-second terminal response time
- On-time delivery for 95 percent of all reports
- An average of n concurrently processing jobs
- An average of less than one percent system downtime
- An average of less than two percent rerun time

These criteria can also be used to obtain early warning signals of potential problems. Trigger points that generate special reports based on the exceeding of predetermined limits can be established. CPU capacity can be governed, for example, by monitoring a system that exceeds 80 percent of CPU time with scheduled jobs for three successive months, achieves less than 90 percent of terminal responses in less than five seconds, operates at an average of more than n concurrent jobs, or averages more than n pages per second as a virtual memory paging rate during normal production. Project progress can be monitored by observing imbalances between project status (percentage complete) and percentage of project funds expended.

Qualitative measures are more difficult to establish. For specific individuals and some groups, objectives that are amenable only to subjective appraisal may be established. For example, the objective of improving relations with user groups is difficult to measure, except by the relative frequency and volume of user complaints. The objective of learning to use a data base management system is also difficult to assess accurately.

Other qualitative measures, however, are amenable to rating or ranking so that subjective appraisals are converted to a quantitative form. For example, although users rarely maintain detailed records of service performance, they build certain perceptions that can translate to scores on a scale. These scales can be used to measure the helpfulness or courtesy of DP personnel or the usability or flexibility of a system.

It is important to distinguish between qualitative measures and measures of quality. The former is concerned with metrics, while the latter implies the existence of some criteria or standards of quality. These implied standards may apply to both qualitative and quantitative measures and criteria.

Such measures of quality focus on products and services. The products of the DP function are usually systems, but they may also include reports or end-user tools. Measures of quality applicable to products include:
- Reliability—Is there regularity, consistency, and dependability in the system or report?
- Usability—Is the system human-engineered to maximize ergonomic characteristics and ease of use?
- Adaptability—Can the product be readily modified to meet changing requirements or ad hoc situations?
- Productivity—Is the product cost-effective? Does it meet anticipated goals?
- Ingenuity—Does the product maximize the use of available resources and technology?
- Innovativeness—Does the product incorporate new methods and techniques or provide opportunities for achieving new benefits?

To some extent, the measures of quality of service overlap the measures of product quality. Reliability, adaptability, and productivity can clearly be applied to services; usability can be applied to only some services. The following measures can also be applied to services:
- Does the service provide adequate capabilities and tools?
- Is the service useful, and is it frequently used?
- Is the service designed to protect itself from the user by minimizing opportunities for end-user error?
- Is the service tolerant of end-user errors and supportive of end-user objectives?
- Is the service available and accessible to the user when needed?
- Does the end user have maximum control of resources consistent with such constraints as available resources and contention from other users?
- Is the service easy for the user to learn and understand? Is it simple in structure and relationships and consistent in design and performance?

TOP-MANAGEMENT REPORTING

The primary objective of the reporting structure is to help top management direct and control the information systems function. The top management of a company usually consists of the president and senior executives, the senior executive to whom the information systems function reports, and/or the corporate DP steering committee.

This top-management group has concerns that should be addressed by the reporting structure, including:
- Problem areas—Reports should point out existing and potential problems and risks. The actual or potential consequences of problems should be clearly indicated.

MANAGEMENT CONTROL REPORTING

- Accountability—Reports should designate the accountability for each function, decision, and project or activity being reviewed.
- Remedial action—Specific action in process or being planned to remedy problems or alleviate their consequences should be presented.
- Variances—Both failure to meet performance objectives and performance exceeding expectations should be reported. Exception reporting is an ideal approach here.
- Benefits—Events or activities that result in benefits should be presented and explained. Individuals should be credited for their contributions to such benefits.

Reports that address these top-management concerns will be more than just a set of charts or graphs. They will contain supporting narrative that interprets graphic material, and they will present other highlights of the operation.

The following reports should be presented to top management and should exhibit the report characteristics for performance control discussed previously. It is suggested that all of the following reports be delivered monthly, except as noted:

- Cost Control Reports
  - Should report the cost of major data centers and total corporate DP costs separately, graphically showing overall budget versus actual expense to illustrate cost trends. Comments should discuss the reasons for trends and variances from the budget.
  - Should summarize cost allocation budget versus actual budget, showing the allocation of costs to users, with comments explaining variances (quarterly).
  - Should show capital expenditures budgeted versus actual (semiannually).
- Resource Utilization (Operations) Reports
  - Available CPU capacity versus capacity used. This report should compare total CPU capacity available with the manner in which all CPU time has been used (downtime, reruns, preventive maintenance, application development, and run time).
  - Available random-access storage capacity versus capacity used.
  - Available data entry capacity (personnel and hardware) versus capacity used.
  - Overtime hours worked by function. This report addresses the use of staff capacity for such functions as operators, control clerks, system programmers, and so on. It signals reaching of capacity limits and the need for added staff or improved work methods.
  - Explanatory comments warning of potential capacity problems or indicating alternatives to improve efficiency or effectiveness.
- Resource Utilization (Systems Development and Maintenance) Reports
  - Backlog of work requests (additions, completions, and cancellations) for new system development, modification requests, and maintenance activity. The backlog should be shown in person-hours (compared

with available hours) and in request count. The percentage of staff devoted to maintenance, modification, and new systems development should be tracked. Average age of requests should be indicated. For priority setting and review, a detailed listing of requests may occasionally be needed by the steering committee (quarterly).
—Status of major projects (i.e., projects above a designated cost level), indicating progress, current status, and problems. This report requirement also appears under performance control (Systems Development and Maintenance).
- Performance Control (Operations) Reports
—CPU time, number of incidents, and cost of recovery for all reruns. These actual counts should be compared with a standard for CPU time and frequency. Comments should explain major causes for reruns and remedial action taken.
—Average and median terminal response time, measured at the terminal, for major online systems versus a standard or objective (bimonthly).
—Reports delivered on time versus a standard (quarterly).
—System downtime versus a standard.
- Performance Control (Systems Development and Maintenance) Reports
—Internal audits on application performance, quality, and so on.
—Status on major projects being monitored, indicating accomplishments versus schedule, cost versus budget, major problems, and so forth.
—Percentage of projects completed on time and percentage completed within estimate for new systems modifications and maintenance (semiannually).
- Performance Control (User Relations) Reports
—Annual survey of user satisfaction with the DP function conducted by a third party (internal audit or a consultant). Such a survey can quantitatively rate DP services by establishing a satisfaction index.
- Resource Allocation Reports
—Cost justifications for major DP expenditures presented for approval to the steering committee and appropriate line management.
—Major proposals for system development presented for approval and assignment of priority. Feasibility studies should support these proposals and be repeated at critical points in the system development cycle.

In addition to the preceding, an annual report can summarize problems or progress in all of these areas and address such items as:

- Over- and underallocation of costs
- Major applications installed
- Major accomplishments
- Benefits obtained for the corporation by information systems (e.g., contribution to profit)
- Long-range plan update
- Objectives for next year
- Annual plan and budget

REPORTING BY THE SENIOR DP EXECUTIVE

The senior DP executive is responsible for the preparation of reports to top management and for collecting the information used to prepare those reports. All information reported to top management is also needed in order to control DP functions. In fact, the same reports are repeated, with some additional technical detail.

This level of report is oriented toward a slightly different set of concerns than the top-management level. Although the focus remains on problem areas, accountability, and remedial action, increased attention is paid to planning factors and to the requirements of daily activities.

In many organizations the senior DP executive holds a weekly staff meeting to supplement the formal reporting system. The formal system would include the following reports, which are monthly unless otherwise indicated:

- Cost Control Reports
  - Detail budget versus actual expense. This report should trigger questions to managers whose organizations show unfavorable variances.
  - Summary cost allocation budget versus actual expense. Variances exceeding the budget by a specified percentage should be explained.
  - Purchase and employee requisitions and contracts should be submitted for approval at this level. In many companies, the senior DP executive approves all DP expenditures, even though they occur within the corporate DP department. This activity occurs as needed.
- Resource Utilization (Operations) Reports
  - CPU utilization reports indicate available capacity versus capacity used. Separate charts for rerun time, downtime, preventive maintenance time, software maintenance time, and internal DP applications run-time use should be prepared.
  - Online system availability. This is a major concern from a user's perspective. The report should track true system availability, the time the system is not available, and the reasons or causes for any lack of availability. These causes may include software, CPU, peripheral, or communications failures. The remaining available time, expressed as a percentage of hours demanded by the user for comparison with a standard, provides a metric for performance evaluation.
  - Computer hours used for program development and testing. The hours should vary in proportion to the program development and maintenance in progress. Discrepancies should be explained in an exception report.
  - Overtime for operations and all other areas should be reported by function so that the need for more operators, programmers, and others or the need for improved methods and procedures can be identified.
  - Deviations from budgeted cost or expected use in supplies. Discrepancies should be explained in an exception report.
  - Data entry use versus capacity available in hours and by percentage.
  - Peripheral device use, indicating time and capacity utilization. This is

reported for planning purposes. The percentage of channel capacity use should also be reported for planning purposes.
- Resource Utilization (System Development and Maintenance) Reports
  —A backlog analysis of work requests showing the number of requests, their estimated work load (in hours), the date of the request, status, and priority. The backlog should be updated (perhaps every 30, 60, or 90 days) and should be reported by user group.
  —Systems development staff time worked versus total available time.
  —Systems development time worked by category (new system development, modification, or enhancement to existing systems and maintenance to existing systems), in hours and as a percentage.
  —Maintenance time (to make a system or program perform according to specifications) and modification time should be tracked over the life of each system to identify candidates for replacement.
  —Detailed monthly project status for all major projects. (This is also a performance control tool.)
- Performance Control (Operations) Reports
  —A summary of reruns by major application, showing frequency, machine time lost, cost of recovery, and cause; this report should help in identifying problem areas. The same data summarized by cause can also be helpful.
  —A summary of the average length of time in job queues and the average number of jobs in the queue. This information provides insight into the effectiveness of hardware management. This data can be separated into statistics for both RJE jobs and internal data center jobs.
  —A summary, by application, of the percentage of reports delivered on time compared to a performance objective.
  —Terminal response time periodically sampled at the terminal. Response time averages and medians should be tracked to detect trends that may result in user complaints.
  —A summary of failures of peripheral devices, terminals, controllers, remote job entry stations, communication devices, and communication lines. These reports can be used to anticipate reliability problems, plan for contingencies, and monitor vendor maintenance performance. The frequency of failures and their causes should be reported.
  —Many users are oriented toward processing of transactions (e.g., insurance companies and banks). Even companies that do not appear to have this orientation require some basis for capacity planning. Transactions processed per month (or per other time unit) and cost per transaction are two excellent measures that can be used to report performance for such organizations. Cost per transaction provides the added benefit of measuring efficiency.
  —Data entry transactions entered compared to a standard by job.
- Performance Control (Systems Development and Maintenance) Reports
  —Percentage of projects completed on time and percentage completed within cost, by project category (e.g., new development, maintenance). If separate development groups exist, this data should be reported for each group.

MANAGEMENT CONTROL REPORTING   63

—Average response time to user requests, separating the time of first response to a system request from the time the work is actually started.
—Average turnaround time for program tests/compilations. This provides a measure of operations support performance.
—Average number of compilations and tests per program. This provides a measure of whether design techniques and tools are being used effectively.
—Two review reports should involve the senior DP executive. The first consists of oral and written design reviews of major or critical systems. The second consists of post-implementation system studies, which should be reviewed with the senior DP executive before final publication.

Functional DP Management Reporting

Functional management reporting is presented to levels of management that include the operations manager, systems development manager, programming manager, and others who report to the senior DP executive. One level may also include first-line supervisors, such as those who supervise data entry, control, library, systems programming, and other functions.

These people either generate reports going to higher-level management or are directly responsible for the production of these reports. In addition, since their performance will be judged on the basis of the contents of these reports, it would be appropriate for these managers to use the information collected in performing their own managerial and supervisory duties.

The concerns of this level of management range from generating the data to its use at a detailed and summary level, including:
- Individual performance evaluation—The information gathered can be used to monitor the performance of individual employees as one basis for their periodic reviews.
- Allocation of personnel—Project control tools can be used to determine personnel availability and assign work schedules.
- Machine performance evaluation
- Ensuring information validity—The data gathered must be validated and controlled. Information reports should have clear audit trails.

Since this level of management works with report details that are summarized for the next higher level of management, the following list only identifies those reports in which the information is put to a use different from other levels of management.
- Resource Utilization (Operations) Reports
    —CPU utilization reports are used directly for initiating remedial action related to apparent problems and for capacity planning. Details can be used for allocating devices to channels or for allocating random-access space. Analysis of peak work load periods may permit work to be rescheduled to maintain reasonable levels of response time.

- —The systems programming function in many organizations reports to the operations manager. It should be noted that the management tools used to control the systems development and maintenance function also apply to planning, directing, and controlling systems programming, communications management, and data base administration.
- Resource Utilization (Systems Development and Maintenance) Reports
  - —Work requests should be logged when received and at each stage of their progress. The log should be reviewed weekly to prevent excessive delays in response time.
  - —Personnel availability schedules should be updated monthly for use in project planning.
- Performance Control (Operations) Reports
  - —Several tools are available for computer performance evaluation (CPE), including job accounting logs, software monitors, and hardware monitors, all capable of providing extremely detailed information for maximizing hardware performance and software efficiency. These tools are recommended for any large computer center. Much of the data required for the performance control reports previously mentioned is derived from these sources.
  - —Reports at this level contain data that can be used for evaluating individual employee performance. For example, data entry transactions keyed by individuals can be compared with job standards. Error rates from verification can be pinpointed. Poor operator practices or poor scheduling can be identified by comparing the average multiprogramming rate with the job queue.
- Performance Control (Systems Development and Maintenance) Reports
  - —Irrelevant measures or measures for which standards cannot be established (e.g., the discredited approach of counting lines of code written) should be avoided. Only meaningful measures should be used for personnel evaluation. These measures include the ability to perform a task on time and within budget, meeting standards for quality and completeness, and appropriately responding to a defined requirement. Project status reports and short interval scheduling for milestone reports can provide this evaluation data.
  - —For supervisors, management-by-objectives techniques can be appropriate performance controls, applied on a semiannual reporting basis.
- Performance Control (General) Reports
  - —A major tool for performance control in any organization is failure reporting and analysis. Problem reports should be filled out for all failures, including machines, programs, power supply, facilities, and so on. These failures should be logged to ensure that follow-up occurs. Failure reports should contain the following information:
    - Problem number
    - Who is reporting the problem (name, location, and telephone number)
    - Date and time the problem was reported
    - Description of the problem (e.g., console data, hardware codes and addresses, serial numbers, system messages)

- Service affected by the problem
- Priority assigned to the solution
- Person assigned to the problem (name, department, and time of assignment)
- Estimated time for solution
- Name of the person making the report

—As the problem is being solved, the following data should be entered:
- Complete description of the problem diagnosis
- Date and time work began on the problem
- Date and time the problem was solved
- Names of all persons who worked on the problem
- The elapsed and actual times devoted to the problem
- Description of action(s) taken to solve the problem
- Description of services affected and the impact on each user
- Action necessary to prevent recurrence of the problem (e.g., work request issued)
- Date and time when the reporter of the problem is notified that the problem has been solved

—Statistics gathered from the problem reports can produce failure analysis reports that pinpoint weaknesses in the organization or its operation.

CONCLUSION

A comprehensive management control reporting system is a major part of any continuing effort to maintain the cost-effectiveness of the DP function. Such a system, emphasizing resource utilization, monitoring, and performance control, must provide information and management control support through all levels of the organization responsible for DP management.

For certain organizations, additional reports may be necessary, beyond those specified. The reports that have been specified apply to centralized, decentralized, or distributed DP organizations, but they may require modification to suit the needs and control objectives of specific organizations.

6 Financial Alternatives for Computer Acquisition

by Paul M. Raynault

INTRODUCTION

The dollar value of computer shipments has been growing at a rapid pace in recent years. This growth has attracted many financial institutions to the computer marketplace; these institutions offer a wide and sometimes bewildering variety of finance options. Some of these options can have disastrous consequences, as some users and large lessors (e.g., ITEL) have already discovered.

The DP manager can profit in many ways by gaining an understanding of different financial arrangements. Such an understanding can give the DP manager:
- A wider choice of ways to acquire equipment and still meet the budget
- The ability to weigh the advantages against the sometimes subtle disadvantages of various options
- The ability to explain the data center's requirements in terms that the organization's legal and financial people can understand

This chapter reviews the five basic financial options available, with emphasis on some of the more common variations. These options are evaluated in terms of the data center business plan, corporate book and tax accounting, and the trade-off between risk and ultimate cost. The calculations throughout this chapter are based on the IRS regulations in effect at the time of publication. The DP manager should consult the organization's financial officer concerning current regulations.

FINANCIAL OPTIONS

For convenience, financial options for DP equipment can be grouped into five reasonably distinct categories:
- Monthly rental from the manufacturer, with no minimum term
- Flexible lease from the manufacturer, usually for two- to four-year terms
- Less flexible (but lower-cost) medium-term operating lease from a third-party financing institution
- Long-term tax-oriented (leveraged) lease from a third party
- Direct user purchase, either with internal funds or financed through the manufacturer or a bank on an installment basis

Financing through the manufacturer (options 1, 2, and sometimes 5) is usually more expensive; however, it is more direct, involves fewer parties, and usually offers less chance of misunderstanding. Similarly, direct user purchase is reasonably well understood. The greatest complications arise in third-party leases (options 3 and 4); however, third-party leases sometimes offer the greatest money savings.

FUNDAMENTALS OF COMPUTER FINANCE

The basic considerations in computer finance are listed in Figure 6-1. As can be seen in this figure, the considerations can be divided into expense and offsetting factors.

	Type of Financial Arrangement	
	Purchase	Lease
Expense	Depreciation Expense	Monthly Payment
Offsetting Factors	Depreciation tax benefits ITC Residual value	Depreciation tax benefits ITC Residual value

Figure 6-1. Basic Financial Considerations

If the DP manager purchases the equipment, the organization's budget will list a depreciation expense, part of which can be recovered through the three offsetting factors listed in Figure 6-1:
- Depreciation tax benefits
- Investment tax credit (ITC)
- Residual value

Depreciation tax benefits result when a company's assets age and decline in value. The actual asset dollars lost through depreciation are an expense of doing business and can be charged against income, thereby reducing tax liability. The new method of calculating depreciation is discussed in a later section.

Investment tax credit (ITC) is a direct tax credit that can be taken by businesses that purchase machinery. The federal government provides the ITC as an incentive to invest capital in expansion, thereby stimulating the economy.

Residual value is the market value of the equipment at the end of its use by the organization.

If equipment is leased (either from the vendor or from a third party), the DP manager's organization will pay a monthly fee for the use of the equipment. The offsetting factors will have a direct effect on this fee—the lessor will reduce the monthly payment according to the value he expects to receive from these considerations. In some cases, the lessor may agree to have the ITC "passed

FINANCIAL ALTERNATIVES 69

through'' to the lessee. (This is usually done when it will improve the lessee's tax picture.) If the ITC is passed through, the lessee must usually compensate the lessor for the loss of this benefit by paying a higher monthly fee. Specific financing options can be analyzed more easily by first reviewing the importance of the offsetting factors.

Residual Value

If the computer is to be installed for a short period (one to three years), residual values often become the dominant consideration in financing, for two reasons:
- Less of the purchase price can be recovered from the initial user over such a short period.
- Except for very old equipment, residual values are high (generally more than 50 percent of cost after two years).

For intermediate terms (three to six years), residual values are still very significant, especially on equipment that has a long expected life in the market.

If the computer will be installed for a long period (seven years or more), the residual value is the least important variable, for three reasons:
- Rapid technological changes ensure that estimates of residual value seven to nine years in the future are for relatively low amounts (0 to 20 percent of cost).
- This value must then be discounted for seven years to compare it with today's purchase price. At interest rates of 12 to 18 percent, this reduces the future value by one-half to two-thirds.
- Because of the high uncertainty associated with estimating residual value over so long a period, most buyers will not count more than 50 percent of any such estimate against current costs.

These three factors usually reduce the contribution of residual value expectations to two to five percent of the cost of the equipment. This figure is usually outweighed by variations in tax benefits, interest rates, and rate variances resulting from vendor competition. Since few users can plan on keeping equipment as long as seven years, however, estimates of residuals are usually very important.

Depreciation Tax Benefits

The tax laws generally provide the same tax benefits to everyone; however, there are two important differences. First, the value of the benefits depends on the recipient's tax rate. For instance, a loss of $1,000 caused by accelerated depreciation will save a corporation $460 (a 46 percent marginal rate); the same loss will save some individuals up to $700 (a 70 percent marginal rate). In contrast, $100 of ITC (10 percent) will save any taxpayer exactly $100 because it is a direct reduction of taxes.

Second, the duration of the benefits is tied to the duration of ownership or use. If a company intends to keep a computer less than five years, it will be unable to benefit fully from the ITC or from depreciation. If that company leases the computer from a third-party lessor, however, the lessor can benefit fully by leasing it to a second user and retaining ownership for a longer period. (Some users who purchase become, in effect, leasing companies; when the equipment is no longer needed, they lease rather than sell it, thus preserving tax benefits. Users who choose this strategy should understand that they are entering a competitive business with its own rules, risks, and rewards.)

In summary, tax benefits are greater for third-party lease than for purchase if the company does not expect to own the equipment for five years, either as a user or by leasing it to a second user after initial use. As a rule of thumb, tax benefits on non-ITC or used equipment are worth about 6 to 10 percent of cost to an investor; this amount grows to 14 to 18 percent of cost if the equipment qualifies for ITC.

Investment Tax Credit (ITC)

The government has made several changes in ITC, most of which have increased its importance in any financing decision. ITC, however, has several unusual features that complicate any analysis.

Direct Tax Reduction. Because the ITC provides a dollar-for-dollar reduction in taxes, it is much more valuable than an equivalent reduction in expense, which increases pretax income. For example, if a corporation has a $1,000 pretax profit, the net profit (based on a 40 percent tax rate) is:

Pretax profit	$1,000
Less taxes	400
Net profit	$ 600

A comparison of the two options—reducing rental expenses by $100 or taking $100 in ITC—clarifies the advantage of ITC. Reducing rental expenses by $100 increases net profit by $60, while pretax profit is raised to $1,100:

Pretax profit	$1,100
Less taxes	440
Net profit	$ 660

Taking $100 in ITC increases net profit by $100, while causing no increase in pretax profit. The tax calculation is as follows:

Taxes	$400
Less ITC taxes	100
Actual Taxes	$300

FINANCIAL ALTERNATIVES

Thus, the profit calculation becomes:

Pretax profit	$1,000
Less taxes	300
Net profit	$ 700

When comparing options involving ITC, it is very important to do all calculations on an after-tax basis.

Size of ITC. The user must claim ITC in the year the equipment is first used or the ITC will be lost. The amount that can be claimed is based on the useful life of the equipment for tax purposes (i.e., the depreciation schedule). The full value of the ITC is currently 10 percent, although this value has changed several times. The full amount can only be claimed if the depreciation schedule actually used is for five years or longer. Under the new tax law, computers have a five-year life, thus qualifying for the full ITC.

Vesting Period. A second rule is used to determine whether the ITC claimed can be kept or whether part or all of it must be returned. This rule is based on how long the equipment is actually kept—the vesting period (see Table 6-1).

Table 6-1. ITC as a Function of Vesting Period

Period Equipment is Actually Kept	ITC Vested (%)
Less than 1 year	0
1 year or more but less than 2 years	20
2 years or more but less than 3 years	40
3 years or more but less than 4 years	60
4 years or more but less than 5 years	80
5 years or more	100

For example, if XYZ buys a $3,000 computer that qualifies for ITC, XYZ is entitled to the full ITC ($300). This reduces XYZ's taxes in the year of purchase. After four years, XYZ decides to sell the computer; but because XYZ did not keep it five years or longer, only 80 percent of the ITC is vested, and the other 20 percent ($60) must be returned to the government. This penalty is an increase in the tax bill for the year of sale.

Who Profits from ITC? The ITC can be claimed by the owner of the equipment, or the owner can elect to allow the user (lessee) to claim it. If the lessee claims it, the vesting period is based on how long the lessee continues to lease the equipment. The lessee does not have to keep using the equipment himself as long as he has a financial involvement (e.g., the lessee can sublease it to another user and still qualify for ITC).

For example, a leasing company purchases a computer and leases it for a three-year term to ABC Company. The leasing company files an election statement allowing ABC to claim the ITC. ABC can then claim the full ITC.

even though the lease is only for three years. At the end of three years, ABC can extend the lease for two more years and sublease the equipment to another user. If, instead, ABC returns the equipment after three years, ABC will have vested 60 percent and will have to refund 40 percent of the ITC on the tax return for that year.

Time Value of ITC. Even if a company does not expect to keep equipment long enough to fully vest, it still gains from the unvested portion because the government does not charge any interest when ITC is not fully vested. In the preceding example, the full ITC was originally claimed, but 40 percent had to be returned after three years. The ABC Company, however, has free use of the money for three years. At today's interest rates, this can be a significant saving.

Discounted After-Tax Cash Flow

The most common method of comparing alternative financing methods is a discounted after-tax cash flow analysis. This method takes into account the effect of taxes, ITC, and the timing of cash flows. (Cash spent today is worth more than cash spent in the future.)

To perform such an analysis, the DP manager must determine two factors—the corporate tax rate and the corporate discount rate. The tax rate will be a composite of federal and local taxes and will depend on the company's profitability.

Discount rate is a calculation of the potential value of money over a period of time. This rate is influenced by borrowing rates and rate of return on investment. For example, the potential investment earnings are lost on a dollar spent today to purchase equipment but are retained on a dollar set aside to be spent in the future to pay for leased equipment. Alternative uses of that dollar must also be considered. A company bases its internal discount rate on these factors. The discount rate will reflect corporate objectives concerning any new investments (not just DP investments).

The actual calculations can be done most easily using a business calculator or a computer program. The following example involves an IBM lease on a 4341-K2 computer; the values used in the calculations are:

Purchase price	$375,000
Monthly lease charge	$ 10,000
ITC useful life	5 years
User's internal discount rate	12 percent
User's marginal tax rate (federal and state)	49 percent

Calculating the true cost over a five-year lease period involves three steps. First, the monthly charge of $10,000 must be discounted at the user's discount rate. On a normal business calculator, the following entries are made:

FINANCIAL ALTERNATIVES

$n = 60$ months
$i = 12$ percent/year $= 1.0$ percent/month
PMT $= \$10,000$/month

Solving for PV (present value) yields $454,046 if the payments are monthly in advance (the most common arrangement) or $449,550 if the payments are monthly in arrears.

Second, this amount is reduced by the tax rate to obtain an after-tax cost:

$$\$454{,}046 - (0.49 \times 454{,}046) = \$231{,}563$$

Finally, the ITC is computed and used to further reduce the true cost. Since computers have a useful life of five years, a user is allowed the full 10 percent of the ITC, based on the purchase price. The ITC equals:

$$0.10 \times \$375{,}000 = \$37{,}500$$

Thus, the discounted after-tax cost is $231,563 - $37,500, or $194,063.

COMPARISON OF FINANCIAL OPTIONS

The two factors that will most influence the choice of financing option are the probable term of initial use and the flexibility required (such as an option to terminate early, to upgrade, or to extend the term). Once decisions concerning these two factors are made, most of the other factors fall into place and the DP manager is left with a smaller choice of financing options. To use an extreme example, a DP manager who can only count on six months of use is unlikely to consider purchase as a practical option. Similarly, if the minimum period of use is seven years, month-to-month rental is impractical. Table 6-2 illustrates how term length and flexibility limit the range of options that should be considered. Each of these three pairs of options can be discussed in greater detail to examine overall economic cost, accounting treatment, and the most significant non-economic factors.

Short-Term Use—Manufacturer versus Third Party

In a short-term lease, the user generally incurs no risks of obsolescence—he pays a higher monthly rate and lets someone else worry about the pace of technological change. From the early 1950s until the early 1970s, this form of financing was almost the only option used, accounting for more than 80 percent of all computers. After declining considerably in importance (to less than 20 percent for IBM's largest computer), this financing method is regaining popularity.

In short-term leases, the DP manager usually specifies a base term and requests that all bidders offer a "clean walk away" operating lease with no guarantees or purchase requirements at the end of the specific term. In such cases, the analysis is very simple—a straight comparison of monthly charges.

Table 6-2. Options as Determined by Term and Flexibility Required

Requirements	Options to Compare
Short-term use and high flexibility	Compare the manufacturer's lease plans to a third-party short-term operating lease.
Medium-term use and moderate flexibility	Compare various third-party options, from short-term operating leases to long-term tax-oriented leases.
Long-term use and lower flexibility	Compare outright purchase with third-party long-term tax-oriented leases.

The lowest third-party rate is compared with the manufacturer's monthly charge. Users generally require at least a five percent savings over the manufacturer's rate to outweigh the normal inconveniences of dealing with a third party. In addition, some vendors (notably IBM) allow the user to claim the ITC directly, even on a short-term lease. Most third-party leasing companies retain the ITC, thus allowing them to offer the user a much lower lease rate—typically 10 to 15 percent below that of the manufacturer.

In the following example, a user requires an IBM 4341 computer for two years. The IBM prices are:

IBM two-year lease (including maintenance)	$ 10,600
Purchase price	385,000
Monthly maintenance	500

A typical two- or three-year third-party net lease should be approximately $9,100 per month, offering savings of $1,000 per month, even with maintenance charges included. In addition, if the equipment is new and qualifies for ITC, then the analysis (described in a later section) comparing ITC options should be used.

Medium-Term Use—Leasing Alternatives

Most users can plan to keep their equipment for only an intermediate term. For them, the choice of financing option is strongly influenced by one decision: Should they sign a lease for the minimum term they can justify and then negotiate lower optional renewal rates if they keep the equipment longer, or should they sign for a longer term to reduce their monthly rate and negotiate for an early termination option?

On most longer-term leases, the best early-termination arrangement a user can obtain is the right to sublease the equipment to a second user. The original user must then make up any shortfall if the new lease rate is lower than the original rate. Signing for a longer-term lease guarantees lower rates because the user is accepting more of the risk of obsolescence. Conversely, short-term leases are at much higher rates.

FINANCIAL ALTERNATIVES

The first step in deciding between these options involves a cash flow analysis that highlights the true cost of playing it safe rather than taking a risk. The actual decision, however, depends on two less tangible questions:
- What is the probability that the equipment will actually be kept longer?
- How important are short-term cost reductions compared with the risks of being wrong?

A detailed financial comparison of these options is provided in a later section.

Long-Term Commitment—Lease versus Purchase

A user may consider making a long-term commitment, for two reasons:
- The user may be able to plan far enough in advance for the equipment to be used for the entire term by only the user's firm. This may involve moving it to different locations during the period.
- The user may be willing to take a risk on the equipment's value after his initial use. This decision requires careful study—many companies make this decision with little forethought and are often unpleasantly surprised when they try to dispose of their equipment.

In either case, the user makes a lease-versus-purchase decision by comparing the two benefits of ownership—tax benefits and the residual value of the equipment—with the lower direct costs of leasing. This comparison is best done on a traditional discounted-after-tax cash flow analysis. Examples are provided in a later section.

Comparison of Various Lease Options

If a user expects to keep equipment approximately four years, he can sign a three-year lease at a higher rate or a seven-year lease at a very low rate. If the equipment is new, the user can ask that the ITC be retained by the lessor; alternatively, the user can pay a higher lease rate and have the lessor pass through the ITC. These two decisions (resulting in four options) must be analyzed to determine the total costs that will result if the user keeps the equipment three years or five years. Eight calculations are thus required.

As discussed previously, the most important variable is the user's estimate of the residual value after three or five years. To be prudent, the value used should be approximately one-half of the best estimated residual value. For example, if the following figures are used

Cost of equipment	$ 375,000
User's discount rate	12 percent
User's marginal tax rate	49 percent

the monthly lease charges will be those shown in Table 6-3. At the end of the three-year lease, the rate drops to $5,000 per month if the lessee wishes to extend the lease for two years.

Table 6-3. Comparison of Lease Charges

Term	ITC Lessor $	ITC Lessee $
3 years	8,090	9,430
7 years	5,320	5,990

On a seven-year lease, the user who wishes to terminate early must estimate how much the equipment can be subleased for during the remaining portion of the lease. In this example, the user estimates that the equipment will have the following residual values after three and five years until the end of the seven-year commitment:

After three years, a four-year lease will be $4,800 per month
After five years, a two-year lease will be $4,100 per month

As mentioned previously, these values should be cut in half. The cost of each of the eight options can then be easily established.

1. Three-year lease, ITC to lessor:
Monthly rate	$ 8,090
Tax at 49 percent	3,640
Net cost	$ 4,450
PV for 36 months	$135,318

2. Three-year lease, ITC to lessor, two-year extension:
Monthly extension rate	$ 5,000
Tax at 49 percent	2,450
Net cost (cost from month 37 to month 60)	$ 2,550
PV for 24 months (value at end of initial 36-month term)	54,712
PV to year 0 (value 36 months earlier)	38,240
Total cost:	
Three-year lease cost	135,318
Two-year extension cost	38,240
	$173,558

3. Three-year lease, ITC to lessee:
Monthly rate	$ 9,430
Tax at 49%	4,621
Net cost	$ 4,809
PV for 36 months	146,235
Value of ITC (claimed)	37,500
ITC returned (40%)	15,000
PV (value today of returned ITC)	10,484
Net value of ITC	$ 27,016

FINANCIAL ALTERNATIVES

Net Cost:	
Three-year lease	$146,235
Net value of ITC	27,016
	$119,219

4. Three-year lease, ITC to lessee, two-year extension (ITC calculation changes from option three because full ITC is vested over five years):

Net cost:	
Initial three years (see option 3)	$146,235
Two-year extension (see option 2)	38,240
	$184,475
Less ITC	37,500
	$146,975

5. Seven-year lease, ITC to lessor, terminate after three years:

Monthly rate	$ 5,320
Tax at 49 percent	2,607
Net cost	$ 2,713
PV for 84 months	$155,236
Sublease rate after 36 months	$ 4,800
Discount for uncertainty	50%
Value to use for analysis	$ 2,400
Tax at 49 percent	1,176
Net income	$ 1,224
PV for 48 months	$ 48,945
PV to year 0	$32,811
Total cost:	
Seven-year lease cost	$155,236
Four-year sublease income	32,811
	$122,425

6. Seven-year lease, ITC to lessor, terminate after five years:

Sublease rate after 60 months	$ 4,100
Discount for uncertainty	50%
Value to use for analysis	$ 2,050
Tax at 49 percent	1,005
Net income:	$ 1,045
PV for 24 months	$ 22,432
PV to year 0	$ 12,348
Total cost:	
Seven-year lease cost (see option 5)	$155,236
Two-year sublease income	12,348
	$142,888

7. Seven-year lease, ITC to lessee, terminate after three years:

Monthly rate	$ 5,990
Tax at 49 percent	2,935
Net cost	$ 3,055
PV for 84 months	174,786
Less full ITC	37,500
Less sublease income	32,811
Total cost	$104,475

8. Seven-year lease, ITC to lessee, terminate after five years:

Seven-year lease cost (see option 7)	$174,786
Less full ITC	37,500
Less sublease income (see option 6)	12,348
Total cost	$124,938

A comparison of these eight options is included in Table 6-4. As is clear from this table, the seven-year lease with the ITC passing to the lessee offers the lowest cost, whether the equipment is kept for three years or five years. Other examples will lead to different results after various terms, requiring the user to decide which term is most probable. In general, leases passing the ITC to the lessee usually offer the lowest discounted-after-tax cash flow.

Table 6-4. Comparison of Eight Leasing Options

Options	Initial Term	ITC	After 3 Years $	After 5 Years $
1, 2	3 years	Lessor	135,318	173,558
3, 4	3 years	Lessee	119,211	146,975
5, 6	7 years	Lessor	122,425	142,888
7, 8	7 years	Lessee	104,475	124,938

DEPRECIATION

Prior to the Tax Reform Act of 1981, there were several depreciation methods. Under the new tax law there is only one method for depreciating computer equipment, no matter what month the equipment is purchased. The new depreciation schedule is 15 percent the first year, 22 percent the second year, and 21 percent the third, fourth, and fifth years.

LEASE-VERSUS-PURCHASE ANALYSIS

A different format must be used for a lease-purchase comparison. Lease and maintenance payments are monthly expenses, while depreciation is a yearly calculation.

For this type of analysis, a yearly spread sheet can be calculated, and then all the yearly costs must be discounted to year 0 (the beginning period). An IBM

FINANCIAL ALTERNATIVES

4341 is again used as an example. The user wants to compare the purchase option with the seven-year lease described previously. To illustrate how a yearly spread sheet is developed, the seven-year lease costs (ITC to lessee, $5,990 per month) described previously are recomputed on a yearly basis, as illustrated in Table 6-5.

The cumulative total cost to year 0 is $174,786, the same value as that computed in the previous analysis of leasing alternatives. From this figure is subtracted the $37,500 of ITC, for a net cost of $137,286.

Using the same yearly format, purchase costs after tax can also be computed (see Table 6-6). Depreciation (described in the previous section) is used on a yearly basis; however, tax benefits are usually claimed on the tax return filed the year after they occur. So in this analysis, depreciation must be offset by a year. The cumulative value in this example is $131,440.

Table 6-5. Seven-Year-Lease Costs Computed Yearly ($)

Year	1	2	3	4	5	6	7
Lease Charge	5,990	5,990	5,990	5,990	5,990	5,990	5,990
49% Tax	2,935	2,935	2,935	2,935	2,935	2,935	2,935
After Tax	3,055	3,055	3,055	3,055	3,055	3,055	3,055
PV for 12 Months	34,727	34,727	34,727	34,727	34,727	34,727	34,727
PV to Year 0	34,727	30,818	27,350	24,272	21,540	19,115	16,964

Table 6-6. Purchase Cost after Tax ($)

Year	1	2	3	4	5	6	7
Depreciation	NA	56,250	82,500	78,750	78,750	78,750	0
49% Tax Benefits	NA	27,562	40,425	38,587	38,587	38,587	0
PV to Year 0	NA	24,460	31,837	29,969	23,934	21,240	0

Note:
NA Not applicable

One of the benefits of ownership is being able to sell the equipment for some residual value. In this example, the user assumes a relatively high value of 20 percent ($75,000 pretax or $38,250 after-tax). This is discounted to a PV of $16,582. Again, because of uncertainty, this figure should be reduced by 50 percent to $8,291. The net cost of purchase is thus calculated as follows:

Cost	$ 375,000
Discounted tax benefits	131,440
ITC	37,500
Discounted residual	8,291
Net cost of purchase	$ 197,769

Although results will vary for other examples, in this example purchase is $60,483 more expensive than net lease costs:

Seven-year discounted after-tax lease cost	$ 174,786
ITC	$ 37,500
Net cost of leasing	$ 137,286

CONCLUSION

The many financial options for computer acquisitions are summarized in Table 6-7.

Several examples in this portfolio were developed using typical lease rates. (These examples are summarized in Table 6-8.) Actual rates vary, based on tax laws, interest rates, and residual assumptions; thus, these examples only illustrate the techniques. The DP manager considering leasing should contact the lessor to determine actual rates.

Table 6-7. Financial Options

Term of Use	Flexibility	Owner	Type of Financing	Whole Risk	Account
3 to 18 months	High	Manufacturer	Monthly rent	Manufacturer	Operating
2 to 5 years	High	Manufacturer	Flexible lease	Manufacturer	Operating
2 to 5 years	Medium	Third party	Operating risk lease	Third party	Operating
6 to 9 years	Low	Third party	Tax-oriented lease	User	Capital/operating
6 to 9 years	Medium	User	Cash/loan	User	Capital

Table 6-8. Summary of Leasing Examples

Owner	Term	ITC	Monthly Charge ($)	Discounted After-Tax Cost		
				After 3 Years ($)	5 Years ($)	7 Years ($)
Vendor	2 years	User	10,600	NA	NA	NA
Third party	3 years	Lessor	8,090	135,318	173,558	NA
Third party	3 years	User	9,430	119,219	146,975	NA
Third party	7 years	Lessor	5,320	122,425	147,888	155,236
Third party	7 years	User	5,990	104,475	124,938	137,286
User	NA	User	NA	NA	NA	197,769

Note:
NA   Not applicable

Only by taking time to compare these alternatives can the DP manager answer the key financial questions:
- Which method is truly the least expensive for the company (rather than which provides the lowest monthly charge)?
- How important is short-term flexibility compared with taking a risk on residual value?
- Are tax benefits important enough to justify purchase over lease?

The key variables connected with these questions are:
- How long will the equipment be usable in the organization?
- What is the corporate marginal tax rate and the internal discount rate?
- After initial use, what will the equipment be worth on a sale or lease?

FINANCIAL ALTERNATIVES

Of these three variables, DP management can best judge the first; others in the organization are responsible for the second. The third variable is equally important, but it is unlikely that anyone in the company has the forecasting expertise needed to supply the answers. Outside help should thus be used in establishing residual values. Help is available from three sources—trade publications, general computer consultants, and companies specializing in computer financial arrangements.

7 User Chargeback

by William E. Sanders

INTRODUCTION

To define DP chargeback systems, it is necessary to describe the evolution of the DP function and to understand some basic principles of cost accounting. In the classic example, the DP function was originally part of the accounting department. At that time, the primary purpose of the computer was to automate financial recordkeeping. The cost was considered part of the expense of running the accounting department.

As the value and function of the computer became better understood, its use was soon applied to other areas of company business. Consequently, the costs associated with DP were shared among users. Allocating costs was quite simple before the advent of multiprogramming. Logs were kept by hand, and costs were shared by dividing total cost by the number of hours of use, as measured by a wall clock, and charging each user for a prorated share. This was the DP chargeback system in its most elementary form.

The process became more complex as multiprogramming evolved. Multiprogramming provided the means to use previously wasted CPU cycles that were lost when a system awaited the completion of an I/O operation. Usage records could no longer be maintained by manual time recording. More sophisticated methods involving the computer's monitoring and recording its own use were needed and were developed.

Today, a comprehensive and accurate way to measure use of a large group of system resources (e.g., CPU time, disk and tape I/O counts, and print lines) exists for most mainframes and operating systems. Many organizations employ these capabilities to charge in-house users for their share of the costs.

Deciding on the resources for which to charge, determining the rates to be used, and having an appropriate system to handle the recordkeeping are the essential steps in setting up a DP chargeback system. These items are the subject of this chapter.

DP AS A CHARGED-OUT COST CENTER

Corporate accounting can view DP either as an overhead function or as a charged-out cost center. When treated as overhead, the costs of DP are not charged directly to the user departments. Rather, they become part of corporate overhead, which may or may not be allocated to the various profit centers within the company. The basis for cost allocation is generally indirect and not based on any measurement of use of services.

Occasionally, DP is treated as a profit center, providing services to its customers at a profit. Customers can be in-house users or outsiders. Although this chapter is written mainly from the perspective of treating DP as a cost center serving in-house users, many of the ideas discussed here can be applied to profit center situations.

Treating DP as a charged-out (or absorbed or allocated) cost center involves taking some or all of the DP department's incurred expenses and directly charging other departments or operations for them, according to some scheme or formula. The costs thus charged then show up directly in the profit and loss statement of the user department and are generally viewed in the same manner as if they were incurred outside the company.

DP costs can be allocated to achieve either full or partial recovery. In a full recovery approach, the objective is to zero out the costs incurred by the DP organization through charges to users. With partial recovery, some portion of the incurred DP expenditure intentionally remains unallocated.

Full-Recovery Approach

In a full-recovery approach, the objective is to zero out the cost of the DP cost center; thus, every dollar of expense must somehow be assigned to DP users. The easiest way to achieve this is to identify the services, units of work, resources, and other items for which a charge is to be made and to treat them as a product line. Cost accounting techniques are applicable in determining the direct and indirect costs associated with each item. Any cost expected to be incurred in running the operation is included in either the direct or indirect category. Rates or unit charges for each item (e.g., resource or service) are determined by dividing the total cost to be recovered for the resource or service (direct and indirect) by the expected use of that resource or service.

In theory, this method of rate setting results in full recovery of costs. In practice, however, this is not the case. Neither the budget/forecast of costs to be incurred nor the estimate of anticipated resource use will ever be exact. The better these estimates are prepared, however, the less the result will vary from a zero balance. There are two methods that can be used to achieve the zero balance desired in the full recovery approach.

Accept a Non-Zero-Balance Condition. The amount unallocated will generally be small relative to the amount charged out. It is equally likely to exceed or undercut the costs. If this approach is adopted, the company should abandon the objective of totally absorbed costs and treat the difference between the amount spent and the amount allocated as corporate overhead. The difference would then be allocated indirectly, pooled with other overhead, or dealt with according to any other company policy addressing corporate overhead.

Force a Zero-Balance Condition. This is accomplished by an after-the-fact adjustment (either a refund or an extra allocation). This can be done monthly if zeroing out each month is important to the company or less often if it is not. It is preferable to make this adjustment less often than monthly since month-to-month fluctuations will occur. If an after-the-fact adjustment is used, there are several ways to determine the amount by which each user's charges will be adjusted. The easiest and most equitable approach is to prorate the amount of refund or extra charge, based on the portion of the total allocation that each user's share represents.

Partial-Recovery Approach

Partial recovery is more complicated than full recovery because it is designed to recover only a portion of DP's costs. While there are two primary reasons for adopting this approach, the effect of both is the same: part of the DP costs are not charged back.

One reason an organization might adopt this approach is that it feels a charge should be made only for direct costs; overhead or indirect cost is not intended to be recovered. In charging for a programmer's services, for example, only the actual hourly salary of the programmer (probably increased by the cost of direct employee benefits and employer taxes) is charged. Not considered are space costs, utilities, supplies, management expenses, and so on, which would be viewed as departmental overhead expenses not to be recovered through use charges.

The second reason for adopting a partial-recovery approach is that the organization feels that some services performed by the DP department should be charged, while others should not. A large insurance company in the West, for example, charges user departments for computer processing and data entry services but not for systems and programming services. In a nearby aerospace company, a slight variation of this practice is the case. The aerospace company charges for processing services but not for systems development. Programming services associated with the maintenance of a system after it has been completed and accepted by the user are, however, charged. The variations are numerous; however, rarely does a company implement a chargeback system and not charge for production services.

The decision on which functions to charge out will be closely tied to management philosophy and corporate policy. This decision can be brought into focus by examining the reasons for a DP chargeback scheme.

Reasons for DP Chargeback

A DP chargeback system helps to state costs accurately, prevent unjustified services, ensure DP department cost-effectiveness, and ensure prudent use of resources. The system can thus benefit user departments as well as DP.

To Accurately State the Total Costs of User Departments. As information processing becomes inextricably interwoven with the operations of most corporate departments and functions, failure to include the costs of processing in user departments' profit and loss statements can be a material distortion. Management risks coming to wrong conclusions in making decisions based on cost or net profit levels of an operation that uses central DP services if the cost of those services is not contained in the total cost of the operation.

To Serve as a Check and Balance against Providing Unnecessary or Unjustified Services. If user departments must pay for services, the organization must help ensure that only necessary and justifiable systems will be developed and operated. Charging for a service is the best way to avoid requests for unnecessary or unjustified work. A DP chargeback scheme is no guarantee against such requests, however; other devices, such as management review committees and cost/benefit analysis, are also needed.

To Help Ensure That DP Functions in a Cost-Effective Manner. When DP costs are charged back to the user departments, some check and balance on DP expenditures is achieved. Although users generally do not see the details of the DP budget, they are prone to compare the costs of in-house services with what they would pay outside. If the amounts charged for DP services fully recover the costs incurred to provide those services, the DP manager who spends money unwisely will soon receive pressure from users who must bear the expense. This is an important reason for adopting a charge-out approach that recovers all, or nearly all, of the DP department's operation costs.

To Encourage People to Judiciously Use Certain Resources. The principles of economics can be effectively applied to managing the demand for resource use. By placing a high price on one resource relative to another (e.g., prime-shift versus nighttime processing), the organization can alter user demand for a particular resource and create a better balance in the use of available capacity. At times, it may be best for the company to discontinue the availability of a certain resource. A sufficiently high price on a resource often leads users to discover alternatives. This is generally preferable to a unilateral discontinuance of the function by the DP manager.

CHARGING FOR SYSTEMS AND PROGRAMMING

If a company employs a chargeback system at all, it will generally accept its applicability to data center operations (computer processing, data entry, and so on,) but will be uncertain about systems and programming. Some advantages and disadvantages of charging for systems and programming follow.

Advantages

Preventing Unnecessary Systems. Charging for development programming services can be one of the most effective safeguards against the development of systems that are unwarranted from a business standpoint. A department generally will not request a project for which justification is lacking if it must bear the cost. Having a management review committee to approve and set priorities for new development projects can help ensure that only justified projects are undertaken. A department head who is politically adept can, however, push his or her pet projects through, unjustified though they may be. This is less likely to occur when the department bears the development expense.

Enhancing Project Control. The decision to charge for services results in the need for a system to record the data needed for charging (i.e., time utilization by the programming staff). This is a benefit. This information is extremely valuable in controlling projects, thus providing management with information on programmer time use and permitting the maintenance of historical data that is useful in estimating. Generally, an automated project control system is used for this purpose. Many good ones are available for purchase.

Improving Productivity. The discipline required for capturing time use by programmers can actually improve the effectiveness and productivity of the staff. This occurs as programmers, accountable for how they spend their time, become more aware of wasted time and how it affects them, their projects, and their users. A tendency to minimize controllable nonproductive time generally results.

Handling Costs for Outside Services. Most companies use or contemplate using outside services at some time. A chargeback system facilitates handling the costs for these services; costs can be easily passed along to the requesting department, since it is already accustomed to being charged for services of this type. A chargeback system also enables a continuing comparison between the cost of in-house and outside service that is useful to DP management.

Disadvantages

Increased Overhead. There is overhead involved when maintaining a chargeback system, adding to the administrative cost of running the DP department. Operating a chargeback system requires software, hardware, and people; depending on the system's scope and complexity, the cost can be significant.

Discouraging Progress. Although discouraging unneeded work is beneficial (as pointed out earlier), desirable activity is sometimes discouraged among users who are too cost-conscious and who do not wish to spend money unless absolutely necessary. This problem can be avoided by routinely using an objective cost/benefit analysis procedure for proposed projects.

Interdepartmental Conflict. Some conflicts with user departments are unavoidable in the chargeback environment. Differences of opinion arise on what a given project should cost, and the inevitable cost overrun is certain to cause heated discussion. Both of these problems can be overcome through the use of good and consistent estimating and project control techniques.

Loss of Control over Programming Personnel. Users paying for the services of a programming staff may consider programmers "their people." This tendency can make it difficult for DP to make or control staffing changes. If the manager responsible for programming is not strong and able to resist user interference, chaos can result.

In one case, a manager with a staff of approximately 50 soon found himself in such a predicament. His organization used a full-recovery system and charged for all programming. Two user departments were very militant about programmer staff changes and insisted on investigating a new member before accepting him or her into one of their project teams. These departments also would not permit the removal or rotation of a staff member they wished to keep. Because they were paying the bill, they felt they had this right, and the programming manager thus lost an important element of management—control.

A related problem arises when users realize they are paying for the salaries and direct costs of their project team and also contributing to the general upkeep and overhead of the DP department. User management may decide to put the programmers on their staff in an effort to reduce costs. If this problem is not controlled, the future of the central DP department is threatened. At this point, senior management may need to reiterate company policy and reestablish equilibrium.

Generally, the benefits of including systems and programming in the chargeback process seem to outweigh the drawbacks. If a chargeback system is adopted, it should include the systems and programming function.

OBJECTIVES OF A CHARGEBACK SYSTEM

Having explored some of the reasons for a chargeback system, the objectives to be achieved in implementing a system will be examined. Meeting these objectives is important in ensuring that the chargeback system will be effective and well accepted.

Fairness. An effective system treats all users equitably. Rates, methods of charging, and so on must be arrived at in an objective manner. One user or group of users must not be subsidized at the expense of another. In a large manufacturing company, for example, all computer-prepared reports were priced according to the number of pages produced—except for the controller's department, which paid a flat $12 per report, far less the amount charged on a per-page basis. Because the controller had clout, this unfair arrangement continued, to the chagrin of other users.

Stability. Once established, the chargeback system must be permitted to change over time. Changes are necessary, as the environment and the use of DP change. System evolution should be gradual. Marked changes monthly and yearly in users' costs should result from changes in use rather than from changes in the chargeback system.

Understandability. The system must be comprehensible to those who deal with it. This is the most important characteristic of a good chargeback system. Concepts need to be kept simple, and the user must be able to understand how charges are calculated. For example, some chargeback systems have attempted to convert all resource use to a common unit of measure, sometimes referred to as the System Resource Unit (SRU) or Common Resource Unit (CRU). Under this approach, a user's bill shows only the number of SRUs or CRUs used rather than the actual resource utilization (e.g., CPU hours, print lines, disk I/Os). This approach fails the test of understandability since the user does not know precisely what the charges are for or how they have been calculated.

Flexibility. This is a characteristic more of those managing the system than of the system itself. The system must not be allowed to become a master to be served; rather, it must be seen as a tool of the organization. As such, the system must be flexible and should change as needed to adapt to the needs of the organization.

Perspective. The purpose of the system should be kept in perspective. The amount of time, effort, and cost invested in its operation should be in balance with the size of the company and the importance attributed to the system.

IMPLEMENTATION OF A CHARGEBACK SYSTEM

Certain steps must be taken to implement a chargeback system successfully. These steps represent a comprehensive approach to doing the job. Shortcuts or modifications to the method can be made, however, and will be noted in the following discussion. The steps are:
1. Develop a DP department budget.
2. Decide which resources will be measured and costed.
3. Estimate maximum and anticipated use levels for each resource.
4. Decompose budget and allocate to cost pools.
5. Calculate resource use rates.
6. Select unit costing or resource method as basis for charging.
7. Develop unit rates for applications using unit costing.

Figure 7-1 shows functions found in most DP departments. Neither the structure nor the function within the organization is important, nor are they intended to be representative of any particular management philosophy. The chart serves only to illustrate some of the points of this section.

Step 1: Develop a DP Department Budget

Since the objective is cost recovery, the budget or expenditure plan for the year must be prepared so that anticipated costs are identified in advance. The DP department can prepare a single budget covering all functions, but the chargeback scheme can be more easily developed if a separate budget is prepared for each functional area.

An organization using the partial recovery approach sometimes chooses to set rates on an arbitrary basis (e.g., competitive rates in the area) rather than

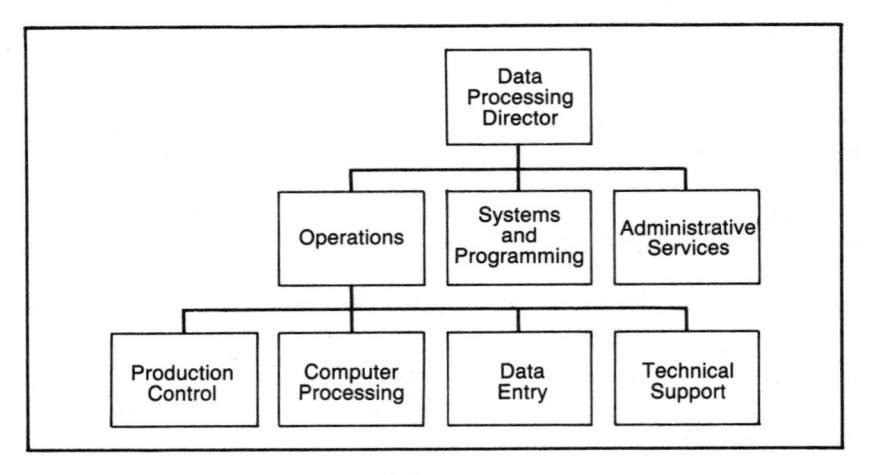

Figure 7-1. Sample EDP Department Organization Chart

base charges on actual costs. If this is the case, a budget is not required for the chargeback process, and steps 1 to 4 are unnecessary. Figure 7-1 shows a sample DP department; Table 7-1 is an example of a DP departmental budget.

Step 2: Decide Which Resources to Measure and Cost

The development of a DP chargeback system is an evolutionary process; its use also evolves over time. Most users of a system that has been in use for any appreciable period can probably see significant differences between the current system and the original.

One element that often changes is the resources that are charged. Choosing well at the outset can reduce the need for later change, but some change is inevitable.

Although it is not necessarily a good approach to charge for whatever can be measured, sometimes a resource is included in the chargeback scheme for no better reason. It is best to ask what the result would be if the particular item were excluded. If an inequity would result and a fair allocation would be impossible, then the resource most likely belongs in the set of chargeable items. The goal is to develop a scheme that levies charges to each user fairly, based on the cost of providing services. It also should be as simple as possible to administer.

Table 7-2 contains a list of resources and a likely unit of measurement for each. It is neither an all-inclusive list nor a recommended one but is intended to show representative resources that can be found in typical chargeback systems.

Step 3: Estimating Resource Use Levels

Estimating resource use levels is a preliminary to Step 6, setting rates. If a chargeback system is based on charging for use of resources at a unit rate, achieving dollar target objectives for the chargeback depends on accurately

USER CHARGEBACK

Table 7-1. DP Department Budget

	A Product Control $	B Computer Processing $	C Data Entry $	D Technical Support $	E Systems and Programming $	F Administrative Services $	Total DP $
Salaries	150,000	400,000	200,000	100,000	800,000	75,000	1,725,000
Benefit Costs	45,000	120,000	60,000	25,000	200,000	22,500	472,500
Rent	15,000	45,000	15,000	4,500	45,000	6,000	130,500
Utilities	0	10,000	2,000	0	0	0	12,000
Hardware Rental/Depreciation	0	500,000	30,000	0	25,000	2,500	557,500
Hardware Maintenance	0	40,000	2,400	0	2,000	200	44,600
Software License/Rental	0	25,000	0	0	6,000	0	31,000
General Computer Supplies	0	2,000	500	0	0	0	2,500
Tape Purchases	0	15,000	750	0	0	0	15,750
Forms Cost	0	60,000	0	0	0	0	60,000
Travel	0	1,000	0	5,000	20,000	0	26,000
Office Supplies	1,000	2,000	500	500	5,000	2,000	11,000
Services Purchased Outside	0	0	2,400	0	40,000	0	42,400
Total	211,000	1,220,000	313,550	135,000	1,143,000	108,200	3,130,750

Table 7-2. Representative Resources and Associated Units of Measurement

Resource	Unit of Measure
CPU use	CPU seconds
Disk use	I/O operations (thousands)
Tape use	I/O operations (thousands)
Print volume	Print lines (thousands) or pages
Library or data storage (disk)	Megabytes/month
Library or data storage (tape)	Volume/month
Card reader use	Cards read (thousands)
Card punch use	Cards punched (thousands)
Data transmission facility	Communications-line minutes
Main memory use	Kilobytes/second
Data entry services	Operator hours
Systems analysis and programming	Programmer/analyst hours

predicting use. Either of two bases, anticipated actual use or maximum possible use, can be employed to estimate use levels.

The philosophy of setting rates based on anticipated actual use is to have each resource fully recover its costs on the basis of whatever use is made. This means that significant shifts in use require rate adjustments to avoid recovering too much or too little. This approach makes users' costs sensitive to resource utilization by other users. If excess capacity exists in the installation, for example, implementing a major new system will reduce the unit rates and, therefore, current users' costs, since utilization increases while costs to be recovered remain relatively fixed. If a user drops out, however, those remaining must each shoulder a greater share of the total cost.

When setting rates on the basis of maximum possible use, the cost of excess capacity is absorbed internally. Although use levels change, rates remain unchanged since they are based on the theoretical maximum achievable use level for each resource measured. This stability of rates generally is preferred by users over the previous method. If the organization does not object to unallocated costs for excess capacity, this method is the preferable one.

Determining use levels requires access to the statistical data produced by the operating system. Measurement of actual use during periods immediately preceding the implementation of the chargeback system provides the best starting point for estimating future use. Analyzing trends and whatever business planning data the organization has developed to plan for future hardware requirements can also be helpful.

If anticipated actual use is selected as a basis for setting rates, only the one-step process just described is required. If maximum possible use is selected, the further step of determining a maximum for each resource must be taken. It is suggested that, rather than trying to estimate a maximum use level in an analytical manner, current use levels be employed to estimate maximum capacity. For example, if the CPU shows 270 problem program hours per month and it is estimated that the CPU is operating at 75 percent of realized capacity, then 360 problem program hours/month is the maximum (270/0.75 = 360). Approached analytically, the problem could be solved as follows:

USER CHARGEBACK

$$\frac{24 \text{ hrs/day} \times 365 \text{ days/yr}}{12 \text{ months/yr}} = 730 \text{ hrs/month}$$

Hypothetical annual resource use levels are shown in Table 7-3. The estimated percentage of maximum capacity on the CPU should be used for other hardware pools, since in most shops, use of these other resources is proportionate to CPU use.

Table 7-3. Hypothetical Resource Use Levels

CPU Hours	2,100
Tape I/Os	620 x 10
Disk I/Os	800 x 10
Print Lines	500 x 10
Data Entry Hours	35,000
Programmer/Analyst Hours	42,000

Step 4: Decompose Budget and Allocate to Cost Pools

In the discussion of Step 4, Table 7-4 should be used in conjunction with the sample budget in Table 7-1. In this example, charges are to be made for the following resources:
- CPU time
- Tape I/Os
- Disk I/Os
- Print lines
- Data entry operator hours
- Programmer/analyst hours

There are thus nine cost pools: the six mentioned plus two overhead cost pools and the unallocated pool. Each budget line item in Table 7-4 is a matrix entry identified by its grid coordinate referenced in Table 7-1. Table 7-4 shows the cost pool of each budget line item. In some cases, the dollars were divided among more than one cost pool. These situations are highlighted and explained further in Table 7-4. For example, line item 1B in the CPU pool represents a $100,000 allocation of the total computer processing salaries listed in Table 7-1.

Step 5: Calculate Resource Use Rates

This is the process that sets the rate to be charged for each resource. It is a very straightforward step that consists simply of dividing the number of dollars in each cost pool (from Step 4) by the use level for the particular resource (from Step 3).

In this example, the annual resource use levels set in Table 7-3 are divided by the dollars allocated each cost pool in Table 7-4. The rate calculations are shown in Table 7-5.

Table 7-4. Cost Pool Allocations

CPU Pool $		Tape Pool $		Disk Pool $	
1B	100,000[1]	5B	75,000[2]	5B	150,000[1]
2B	30,000[1]	6B	6,000[3]	6B	12,000[3]
5B	200,000[2]	9B	15,000		162,000
6B	16,000[3]		96,000		+ 54,700[5]
7B	25,000[4]		+ 54,700[5]		+ 4,328[6]
	371,000		+ 4,328[6]		221,028
	+ 328,200[5]		155,028		
	+ 25,968[6]				
	725,168				

Print Pool $		Data Entry Pool $		Programmer/Analyst Pool $	
1B	150,000[1]	(1-13)C	313,550	(1-13)A	971,550
2B	45,000[1]		+ 21,640[6]		+ 43,280[6]
5B	75,000[2]		335,190		1,014,830
6B	6,000[3]				
10B	60,000				
	336,000				
	+ 109,400[5]				
	+ 8,656[6]				
	454,056				

Hardware Overhead Pool $		General Overhead Pool $		Unallocated Pool $	
(1-13)F	211,000	(1-13)F	108,200	(1-13)D	54,000
1B	150,000[1]		−108,200[6]	(1-13)D	+ 171,450
2B	45,000[1]		0		225,450
3B	45,000				
4B	10,000				
8B	2,000				
11B	1,000				
12B	2,000				
(1-13)D	+ 81,000				
	547,000				
	−547,000[5]				
	0				

Final Budget Decomposition $

CPU Pool	725,168
Tape Pool	155,028
Disk Pool	221,028
Print Pool	454,056
Data Entry Pool	335,190
Programmer/Analyst Pool	1,014,830
Unallocated Pool	+ 225,450
Total	3,130,750

Notes:

[1] Computer operations salaries and benefits split among CPU, print, and hardware overhead pools, based on analysis of duties.
[2] Hardware expense allocated to pools based on actual equipment assigned each pool.
[3] Hardware maintenance proportionate to hardware expense.
[4] All software allocated to CPU pool.
[5] Hardware overhead allocated as follows: 60% CPU; 10% tape; 10% disk; 20% print (arbitrary).
[6] General overhead allocated as follows: 40% programmer/analyst; 20% data entry; 24% CPU; 4% tape; 4% disk; 8% print (arbitrary).

USER CHARGEBACK 95

Table 7-5. Rate Calculations

CPU	$\dfrac{\$\ 725{,}168}{2{,}100}$	= $345.32/hr
Tape	$\dfrac{\$\ 155{,}028}{620 \times 10}$	= $0.25/1,000 I/Os
Disk	$\dfrac{\$\ 221{,}028}{800 \times 10}$	= $0.28/1,000 I/Os
Print	$\dfrac{\$\ 454{,}056}{500 \times 10}$	= $0.91/1,000 lines
Data Entry	$\dfrac{\$\ 335{,}190}{35{,}000}$	= $9.58/hr
Programmer/Analyst	$\dfrac{\$1{,}014{,}830}{42{,}000}$	= $24.16/hr

Step 6: Select Either Resource or Unit Costing as Chargeback Approach

The resource method consists of measuring the resources employed by each user and computing the bill, using the rate established for each resource. The user thus receives a bill along the following lines:

1.46 CPU hrs @ $345.32	$504.17
6.81 Mi Disk I/Os @ $0.28	$190.68

To many users, such a bill is meaningless and undesirable. Many prefer units that they themselves can measure (to keep DP honest) and for which they can predict volume (useful in budgeting for DP services expenses).

Charging on the basis of item produced or processed (such as number of payroll checks, invoices produced, policies written, or account inquiries) rather than on the basis of resources used is the alternative approach. This approach, called unit costing or standard costing, is described in Step 7.

A combination of the two approaches can be used. For some users or systems, one method may be preferable. As long as the objectives of the chargeback system are met, either approach to calculating a charge for services, if agreed to by user and provider, is acceptable.

Step 7: Develop Unit Rates for Applications Using Unit Costing

This step is optional and is of interest only if the unit costing approach to recovery, defined in Step 6, is to be used.

The objective of the unit costing approach is to recover the same number of dollars that would be recovered using the resource approach but to do it using chargeable items other than resources used. The amount of the bill is not at issue but, rather, the manner in which it is calculated. Some creative cost accounting is therefore in order. The following steps will accomplish it.

Decide Which Units to Use. This requires a careful look at the application system to discover units that are meaningful to the user and easily countable and for which change in resource use is somewhat directly proportionate to change in the unit count. In the trust business, for example, a workable unit is the number of accounts being serviced or processed. While the amount of processing performed is to a great degree dependent on the number of transactions processed, the relationship between accounts and transactions proves to be nearly constant over a somewhat stable group of accounts. Therefore, sufficient correlation between number of accounts and resource use costs exists to use number of accounts as the unit of measure. Furthermore, number of accounts is preferable to number of transactions because it is easier to count and simpler for the user to understand and to predict in advance. More than one unit of measurement may be required to sufficiently express processing costs in meaningful application units. For example, the amount of processing for the application might be highly dependent on both transaction count and number of statements produced. In this case, both items should be used as chargeable units.

Establish the Relationship between Number of Units and Resource Cost over a Period of Several Months. Several readings must be taken to set a unit rate. The objective is to recover the same amount by the unit method as would have resulted from the resource method. Table 7-6 is an example, using just a single unit.

Table 7-6. Average Units and Resource Costs

Month	No. of Accounts	Resource Cost $
1	5,625	18,721
2	5,700	19,085
3	5,683	18,610
4	5,528	18,302
5	5,632	19,468
Avg	5,634	18,837

Calculate the Unit Rate. Divide the average resource cost by the average number of units. In this example, the average number of units is 5,634, and the average resource cost is $18,837. The average unit cost is therefore $3.34. When using multiple units, establishing the correlation is more difficult, requires more data samples, and is subject to more trial and error.

Validate the Selection of Unit and Rate Calculation. Taking each of the five months in the sample, the results using the calculated rate are shown in Table 7-7.

Table 7-7. Rate Calculations Using Resource Cost and Unit Cost

Month	No. of Accounts	Resource Cost $	Unit Cost (@ $3.34)	% Difference
1	5,625	18,721	18,788	+0.36
2	5,700	19,085	19,038	−0.25
3	5,638	18,610	18,981	+1.99
4	5,528	18,302	18,463	+0.88
5	5,632	19,468	18,811	−3.37
		94,186	94,081	−0.11

In this example, the correlation is excellent. The deviation each month is very small and the total result almost exact. Such precise results will seldom be obtained, and they need not be this good to be workable. A little practice will show whether a proper unit has been chosen.

WHEN TO CHANGE RATES

The decision on how often to change rates is important. Conditions that affect rates change frequently (cost levels, utilization levels, software, and so on). Rates calculated at the beginning of the year to effect the particular recovery philosophy of the installation will probably no longer be adequate by mid-year. Should they be changed at that time?

If the rates being charged are causing excess recovery but are otherwise equitable, they should stand. The excess can be handled at year-end through a refunding procedure, which always pleases users.

If the recovery will fall short of what is needed, there is a choice. Rates may be considered to be a contract with users for the entire year. Having set rates incorrectly, the loss must be absorbed. On the other hand, rates may be seen as subject to change without notice, in which case they should be changed when sufficient justification exists.

"Sufficient justification" is a subjective concept; universal agreement on it may be difficult. Nonetheless, several situations can arise that seem to justify changing of rates, provided the installation has adopted an interim rate-changing policy.

If a major change dramatically altering the costs of providing services occurs in the installation, a rate change is warranted. Examples are a CPU change, migration to new disk technology with significantly different price/performance characteristics, or a major software change resulting in changed resource use.

If a material inequity in charging a user who is on the unit cost method of allocation is discovered, a rate change to that user only is justified. This situation can arise through a significant volume change, an application software change, or inaccurate unit cost setting. Unit rates are generally accurate only within a fairly narrow range of volume; once outside the range, a rate change becomes necessary. Application software changes can have a major impact on the efficiency and resulting resource utilization of an application.

Finally, if the installation does not absorb the cost of excess capacity but sets rates based on actual use, a rate change may become necessary when utilization levels exceed a certain limit. A major new application added during the year and not anticipated when rates are set will cause an excess recovery. A new user, for example, is beneficial to existing users since the new application utilizes excess capacity and thus drives down the rates. Conversely, the loss of some processing volume may cause a rate increase to avoid shortfall. Under any circumstances, changing rates more often than quarterly is probably not justified. It is highly desirable to maintain stable rates for the duration of the normal budget period (usually a fiscal year) if at all possible.

CONCLUSION

Designing and implementing a DP chargeback system requires, initially, setting objectives and deciding the purpose of the system. A 7-step implementation process must then be undertaken in careful detail. The results of such effort can greatly benefit budgeting and productivity in both DP and user departments.

8 Problems in Decentralized Computing

by Larry D. Woods

INTRODUCTION

In recent years, MIS management has been confronted by an increasing number of requests for online processing, data base systems, vaguely defined requests leading to longer development queues, and inquiries from top management about the plans of the MIS department for distributing computing. Two areas associated with these problems need to be examined.

The first area involves computers that are purchased and supported by non-MIS personnel. Although there are valid uses for small computers in non-MIS-controlled areas, there is a great risk that "automation anarchy" can occur. The reality of this situation and the steps for controlling this problem are examined in this chapter.

The second area of concern for MIS management is understanding and evaluating distributed data processing (DDP). Many MIS managers are asking:
- Should we distribute?
- What should we distribute?
- How do we distribute?

In addition, MIS management is frustrated by the confusion of defining distributed data processing (DDP) as well as by the various DDP implementation techniques. The result of this confusion can be called "the distributed data processing dilemma." Thus an analysis of the concept of DDP and a plan for evaluating its effectiveness in a given corporation are proposed in this chapter.

DECENTRALIZED COMPUTING

A decentralized computing system is characterized by autonomous control exercised by non-MIS personnel. This type of control can create an environment where automation anarchy can flourish.

For example, a minicomputer system was purchased to furnish local processing for an engineering department. During the next year, miscellaneous requests were issued for funds in order to purchase "laboratory instruments" and "test equipment." Eighteen months after the system was installed, the MIS department discovered that the laboratory instruments and test equipment were, in fact, add-on peripheral devices for the minicomputer. A data base software subsystem had been installed, and several nonengineering programs had been developed, including two reports for the plant manager.

This type of occurrence is not unusual. Frequently, computer systems are purchased as expendable laboratory equipment, personal computers are purchased from local stores for use in various corporate areas, and computer kits purchased with petty cash vouchers are assembled at home and brought into the plant as finished products. These examples point to a phenomenon that is occurring in many departments in large organizations—local planning and development of computer systems by non-MIS personnel, without the knowledge of the MIS department.

One large pharmaceutical company with centralized DP control recently made a study of its total DP expenditures. To its surprise, only 49 percent of the dollars being spent on DP were under the control of the DP department. The majority of the cost was incurred outside of the central DP environment. Yet, the DP department had been chartered to ". . . control DP expenditures."

THE PROBLEM OF AUTOMATION ANARCHY

With no slight intended, engineers can be used as an example of the problem of automation anarchy. Typically, the DP department justifies its systems expenditures on a dollar basis—no ROI (return on investment), no system. This fact, coupled with the facts that engineering applications are justified by many intangible costs and many data processors lack an engineering background, pushes most engineering projects to the bottom of the development queue.

In the past, such long delays were a "grin and bear it" situation for the engineering department. In the early 1970s, this situation was alleviated for a short time with the introduction of various online development systems, such as ROSCOE and TSO. Although these tools are still being used extensively, the door was closed to many applications when the data base activity was introduced into corporations. The ability to program and develop is still present, but the data is not available. The engineer must again depend on the MIS department for most of his systems development.

This predicament, however, is not an engineering problem alone. The same type of frustration is experienced in marketing departments, part and whole goods distribution areas, and various financial functions.

Today, companies are using much more sophisticated techniques to evaluate such items as market shares, distribution channels, and financial plans. Multinational corporations need tools and systems that can evaluate international monetary conditions. Top management wants financial information at its fingertips. These demands are not frivolous; in many cases, however, they cannot be cost-justified. If the user is fortunate enough to have access to a mainframe, he can develop his own solution. If not, he must go to the DP department with his request, have it added to the development queue, and wait.

The Joys of Computer Ownership

The frustration caused by long delays in developing solutions forced many users to seek alternatives. The minicomputer is one of them. Minicomputer ownership presented the user with a potential solution. The perceived benefits of minis include:
- Low-cost computing
- Total freedom for development
- Ease of programming
- Better computer performance
- Growth potential and flexibility
- Absence of control

Many of these minicomputer attributes may be overemphasized by proponents of minicomputer ownership. Users, nevertheless, are convinced that they *can* run jobs more efficiently and faster on their own computers. The following example is a typical minicomputer success story.

At a large manufacturing facility, a new product was scheduled to go into production in nine months. A potential production scheduling problem was recognized, and a request was made to the MIS department for new system development, namely, programs that would ensure a smooth start-up for this product. The MIS development phase for the new product, however, was scheduled to begin six months later because of existing work loads. Production personnel could not convince the MIS department that this project warranted an urgent rating.

Opting to complete the necessary work in-house, an engineer assigned to a minicomputer was recruited for the task. The programs were developed and tested, and reports were produced in three days. With these reports, production personnel discovered that their production problems were more serious than anticipated and they could avert the scheduling problem with savings that justified the total cost of using the minicomputer for five years.

This example is not unusual, nor is this a solution that could only be accomplished by a minicomputer. It does illustrate that alternatives are available to non-MIS users who believe that they are not receiving adequate service from the MIS department. Problems do not disappear, however, simply because users have access to a computer.

The Problems of Computer Ownership

The potential problems associated with the proliferation of small computers in a large organization, when viewed from the corporation standpoint, are many.

Lack of Direction. Small computers are being installed to serve the needs of small segments of the corporation. Frequently, very little coordination of minicomputer purchases is exercised; thus, the effect on the whole organization of installing one or more small computers is being ignored.

For example, an instrumentation department purchased a minicomputer system to be used as a complex piece of monitoring equipment. The system to be developed around this computer was to be used by other testing departments. Unfortunately, the potential users of the new system were not consulted. The computer system chosen by the instrumentation department was much more expensive than the other users could justify; thus, they had to wait a year before using the system. The primary interest of the developer had been to acquire a computer that met his department's needs, without adequately considering the needs of the other users.

Lack of Local Planning. A computer is installed in an engineering department to perform "engineering computing." A minicomputer is purchased by a financial department to perform "simulations." Generalized descriptions of computer needs can signal poor planning. Users should develop concrete plans or long-term blueprints for the utilization of their computer systems. Lack of planning can create problems associated with escalated usage or with the development of an unanticipated mini data center.

User Naiveté. Usually, non-MIS managers must learn to cope with the added responsibility of a computer. Work descriptions may need to be changed, and work content for many will change. Relations must be established with minicomputer vendors. In addition, as the potential for a full-time systems staff develops, career paths should be considered.

Overlapping System Requirements. People working on similar problems usually solve the problems in a similar fashion. With many computers installed in various departments throughout a large organization, these solutions can be needlessly duplicated in the absence of coordination and control. Usually, very little communication takes place among the various users. This type of problem, of course, may occur more frequently in decentralized organizations. The following situation clearly illustrates the consequences of overlapping system requirements.

A machine tool maintenance system was developed for a multilocation manufacturing facility. The system was to be executed on the host mainframe at Location A. An industrial engineering study determined that certain features of the system could be enhanced by using minicomputers. A subsequent joint study by the DP and the IE departments found that, although initial study findings were accurate, the savings were not great enough to warrant the purchase of additional minicomputers.

Location B had a minicomputer, although it was being used for another purpose. By upgrading this equipment, the machine tool maintenance system rejected at Location A was installed in Location B. This implementation, however, was performed without the knowledge of the DP department at Location B. In addition, Location B staff were unaware that Location A personnel had even considered a comparable system.

DECENTRALIZED COMPUTING

Loss of Data Control. One of the greatest fears aroused by the proliferation of small computers in large organizations is the loss of data control. Most companies identify data as a corporate resource. The value of this data has been recognized; in some cases, an actual dollar value can be assigned to it. The haphazard introduction of computers throughout an organization introduces the possibility of losing control of certain data needed by various people within the organization. Thus, the temptation to store data on one's own computer storage device develops.

A tooling department, for instance, was responsible for maintaining its inventory on a corporate IMS data base. This was being done online through CRTs. Excessive host computer costs, slow response times, and demands that data be available for additional local functions prompted this department to create a duplicate data base on its local minicomputer.

Eventually, it became obvious that too much time was being spent in maintaining the data on both systems. The tooling department opted to discontinue more frequent updating of the corporate data base. Instead, the corporate data base was updated weekly with a batch RJE run from the minicomputer. This decision was made, of course, without the knowledge of the MIS department.

Security. Data stored on minicomputers is often easily accessible to unauthorized scrutiny (at least more easily accessible than it is on the centralized computers with their many levels of security protection).

The non-MIS manager, confronted with the responsibility of computer ownership, usually attempts to handle data security in one of two ways. He either assigns full responsibility for the computer system to one person, thus encouraging a closet-type computer systems department, or yields control of the installation to subordinates, thus risking a laissez-faire mode of operation.

The latter alternative is usually preferred by the non-MIS manager because his superiors warned that he would otherwise become deeply involved with computer operations. The non-MIS manager, therefore, can plead ignorance on problems of data security and hope for the best.

Because so many decentralized computing systems are being installed in diversified areas of large corporations, the immediate reaction of some MIS managers is to impose strict controls. This may be a good short-term solution for the MIS managers, but it may not be a good solution in terms of corporate profitability. One suggested approach is presented after the discussion on the use of minicomputers within the MIS department.

DISTRIBUTED COMPUTING

GUIDE, an IBM mainframe users group, defines distributed computing as, "The logical and/or geographical dispersion of computing nodes, interconnected in a coordinated basis." [1] This definition of distributed data processing (DDP) is used in this chapter.

The GUIDE definition of distributed computing does not include decentralized standalone computers, which are rarely used in a coordinated interdepartmental effort (at least from the viewpoint of MIS management). Thus, a distributed computer should always be considered a functional part of a larger system.

The need for distributed computing has been created by the ever-increasing demand for online systems. If interactive and/or real-time systems were not needed, there would be little need to distribute computing power.

Minicomputers configured into DDP systems are additional tools that the MIS department can use in developing solutions; they can serve as building blocks that can simplify the design of many new systems that the MIS department is asked to produce. DDP solutions can also provide more reliable systems, as will be noted later.

Functionally, the distribution of computing power existed before users started implementing minicomputers for this purpose. The introduction of remote, interactive terminals gave users access to large mainframe power at all workstations. They no longer had to fumble through large volumes of paper in order to obtain information. By simply inquiring through a CRT or teletypewriter, the information required could be obtained. In addition, the data received was frequently more accurate because the data fields were updated as events occurred.

The use of terminals connected to mainframes obviously continues today; problems, however, have surfaced. These problems, which have created the need for distributed computing solutions, are discussed in the following sections.

Reliability

Computers, large and small, do malfunction on occasion. For example, in the batch environment, hardware and software problems often went undetected. Users were buffered from the true computing environment by job entry clerks. Because it was not critical if jobs were not run exactly on schedule, short, nondestructive system outages were tolerated.

The problem of mainframe reliability first surfaced when some large corporations adopted a computer utility concept. In this implementation, computer power was centralized and users installed remote job entry (RJE) stations. With the introduction of RJE stations, a large segment of the user community could view the problems of the host system at the moment they occurred. All of these users felt the impact of the problem simultaneously. The positive side of this situation was that most, if not all, RJE users were DP departments.

One problem with mainframe reliability is software. Undependable software is inherent in a system that is being used to provide general yet diverse computing tools to large segments of a user community.

Software problems can occur both within various components and through the interaction of various software subsystems. In addition, a great deal of the user-created software being considered here can lead to further difficulties.

DECENTRALIZED COMPUTING

As the sophistication of users increases, more software subsystems are required. New factors are introduced—unique combinations of subsystems, some never tried before. Support expertise is required for each new subsystem. These support groups must be coordinated so that the total host system can move in step. To understand these operations, one need only look at the size of the support staffs required for large mainframe computers and the number of software fixes that must be applied to these systems in order to keep them running.

The introduction of online systems also demands more software subsystems that, in turn, create more potential software problems. Simultaneously, more users are exposed to these problems and are affected directly. In the online environment, an idle machine means idle workers. Unlike the RJE environment, however, these users are not DP departments; they are non-MIS users. These points should not be interpreted to suggest that the use of a centralized mainframe computing system is unnecessary or uneconomical. Some observers claim that the large savings of centralized systems are eroding because of necessary support cost. (The merits of this argument are beyond the scope of this chapter.) The point is that there is, and will continue to be, a reliability problem with large host system software and, therefore, a continuing problem with host computers.

Performance

Various elements in a centralized computing system can cause response time to suffer in an online system, as follows:
- External system interference
- System software
- Telecommunications

In a general-purpose system that is executing many diverse tasks simultaneously, interference (i.e., conflicts among system components) will occur. Simultaneous requests for devices or data create a win-lose situation. The CPU and its program memory must also be shared on some form of priority basis. These conflicts can ultimately create delays.

Software subsystems can also cause delays. First, software that must support a general user audience can, by its very nature, contain code that is frequently executed unnecessarily. Second, the levels of software that must be introduced into a generalized system add delays.

Because remote terminals are used for online systems, telecommunication delays can also occur. Response time becomes a function of the speed of the host computer software *and* the speed of the communications link. The delay inherent in the telecommunications line is increased by the use of CRTs, with their capability of displaying large amounts of data. Transferring 1,000 characters to a CRT can take several seconds, regardless of the processing time taken by the host computer.

Expandability and Flexibility

In many applications, small increments of memory or data storage must be added periodically. This expansion capability is not economically feasible on most mainframes but can be accommodated very easily on minicomputers. The minicomputer can provide the means for obtaining fast, reliable, and flexible online systems. The simple hardware and software structures provide a less complicated environment for program execution. Furthermore, these computers are dedicated to either one task or one set of complementary tasks. Consequently, maximum uptime, which is necessary for online system success, can be obtained.

THE PRESENT MIS ENVIRONMENT

Why are MIS departments not including distributed computing systems in departmental plans? The MIS departments of most corporations are oriented toward the use of large computers. This tendency is to be expected because the MIS department is responsible for operating the large mainframes of the corporation. In fact, large computers are the MIS department's raison d'etre.

Assuming that the MIS department has a satisfactory relationship with its mainframe vendor, the department has no incentive to seriously consider the use of small computers. At the present time, no mainframe manufacturer offers a total DDP solution; therefore, there is no support from this direction if an MIS manager chooses to consider DDP.

In addition, systems analysts usually have no training in the design of DDP systems. Their design experience has always been limited to large centralized machines. Many analysts start as programmers who, in most cases, develop programs on large mainframes.

Introducing a DDP solution to a systems problem can also mean entering a mixed-vendor environment. Although many MIS shops use foreign peripherals, there is reluctance to commit to an untried vendor for a totally new system.

There are additional unknown factors. How will the small machine interface with the large mainframe? What problems can be expected with this interface? Equipment performance, unless it can be compared to an existing installation, is an unknown. Reliability and maintenance can also pose problems. Other factors that weigh heavily against DDP are:
- The amount of programmer training needed to develop the system
- The future of trained personnel if DDP projects do not continue
- The level of continuing support for the minicomputer software

In addition, many large organizations have a distributed data base problem. Certain segments of industry depend heavily on integrated data. Distributed data bases are essential to many applications. The tools needed to manipulate distributed data bases are available from some minicomputer vendors. The problem lies in the fact that these data base management systems do not interface with the mainframe manufacturer's DBMS. Special coding must be introduced and maintained.

TOWARD A SOLUTION: COMPUTING COORDINATION

As noted, the use of minicomputers introduces two problems that must be examined by the MIS department. These problems concern, first, the lack of control of decentralized computers within the organization and, second, the lack of the understanding needed to utilize DDP solutions within the development framework of the MIS department.

MIS management should be reconciled to the fact that minicomputers do exist and cannot be ignored. It is essential that MIS management understand the potential of minis. Non-MIS departments will continue to utilize this equipment, regardless of whether the MIS department condones the practice. In many cases, non-MIS department managers look for support and consultation in the acquisition of minicomputers. Currently, their only source is the vendor.

Within the MIS department, DDP solutions offer the potential for more reliable and cost-effective computer solutions, although design considerations may pose problems. The number of offerings of DDP equipment from mainframe vendors and minicomputer suppliers requires sufficient expertise to be able to determine the optimal configuration for a given problem. Creating a computing coordination group can provide much of the expertise needed to assist both the MIS department and non-MIS users.

The coordination group should be responsible for coordinating all computer activity within the corporation. This should include outside time-sharing and RJE services, minicomputer usage, WP activity, personal computers, and the expansion of the central mainframe installation.

Physical size, economies of scale, and programming capabilities of the various computer resources available are causing an overlapping of equipment types. Minis are becoming maxis, maxis are becoming minis, and new types of equipment are becoming more usable for commerical purposes (e.g., the home or personal computer). Thus, it is important that the responsibility for the coordinating of computer usage be accepted by MIS management.

The functions of the computing coordination group should include:
- Coordination
- Consultation
- Software support
- Planning

Coordination. Coordination does not imply control. This is a very important point. The MIS department cannot expect to control the acquisition of all computers within the corporation. This is not to suggest that a laissez-faire attitude should be permitted; instead, users should be given the latitude to design, develop, and maintain their own systems upon receiving approval and within a framework of standards and guidelines developed by the coordination group.

Standards developed for non-MIS users should direct attention to areas of corporate concern. These standards should not emphasize the detailed design and programming techniques used by the MIS department. Instead, such items as data usage and network control standards should be defined. Unduly detailed standards will be ignored by users, unless a strong case is made for their use.

User input in the development of standards should be encouraged. Users should not feel that the standards are being forced upon them. Enforcement of standards, however, should not be a function of the coordination group. This is an internal DP auditing function. Trust in the coordination group should not be jeopardized by assigning any policing responsibilities to it.

Consultation. The coordination group should include a knowledgeable consultant who can be available to non-MIS users who are interested in considering alternative computing power sources (hardware, software, or services) and to MIS analysts or designers who may be considering DDP solutions.

Consultation with non-MIS users should begin at the earliest possible time. It is important that the basis of their need for alternate equipment or service be understood. This should not imply that consultation should become a form of system analysis, although it is important that the user task be properly understood so that adequate advice can be given.

The concept of DDP can be promoted within the MIS department if all project requests are routed through the coordination group before design work begins. At this time, a decision can be made on the potential of a DDP solution for the project. A DDP proposal can then be issued by the computer coordination staff, if one is warranted.

The group consultant must remain objective when dealing with both non-MIS and MIS users. The purpose of consulting is to assist in working out usable computing solutions. This objective must be understood and accepted by both the user and the coordination staff.

Another important consulting service is the vendor liaison activity, which involves acquiring large turnkey projects by incorporating minicomputers in various control functions. Such systems as automated storage facilities, conveyor systems, and central numerical-controlled machine systems fit in this category. Large systems of this type are usually purchased by non-MIS personnel. Although the purchaser may be knowledgeable about the system and its expected results, he may lack technical understanding of the computing equipment and systems that are part of the turnkey product.

The coordination group should represent the corporation in negotiations with turnkey vendors. Their participation should cover both the initial analysis of the proposed system and the development and subsequent installation of the equipment. All work should be performed in cooperation with the purchasing department. In effect, the coordination consultant acts as the user's representative.

Software Support. System software support for all minicomputer systems should be the responsibility of the coordination group. This includes such activities as operating system generations, the installation of ''fixes,'' and the development of general-purpose software (e.g., network software). The coordination staff should not, however, develop application software.

Most minicomputer installations do not require a software staff because their computers basically perform repetitive functions. It has been found that a shared software support staff can easily provide this service to a large number of diverse systems.

Planning. The planning function of the computing coordination group covers many activities. Thus, time should be devoted to studying the trends of the computer industry and its companion field, electronics.

The rapidly growing computer industry offers many acceptable alternatives for solving most current computing problems. The time of the vendor-proposed solution is disappearing. Instead, the vendor offers many products that can be assembled in "building block" fashion in order to provide a workable system. Thus, users must become more responsible for planning their own systems.

New classes of computer devices should be evaluated by the coordination group. Some examples of these kinds of equipment are audio-response units, bar code readers, and voice recognition devices. These types of peripherals are important because minicomputer systems can be adapted easily to them. Knowledge of the availability of various types of peripherals can aid users in developing cost-effective systems.

CONCLUSION

The frustration felt by many MIS managers when they examine the proliferation of minicomputers throughout their corporations can be explained by these factors:
- The typical MIS department lacks knowledge of the implementation of small computers.
- The low price of small computers is causing users to question the high cost of central computing facilities, thus forcing MIS departments to defend a previously accepted position.
- More users are searching for alternatives as they become concerned about the unreliable service being supplied by the MIS department.
- Users are pressuring MIS to cut the development queue wait time.

We are entering the "era of the user." User needs must be satisfied. MIS must take a positive attitude toward alternative computing solutions; when warranted, such solutions should be proposed. This is the time for an aggressive, service-directed approach. Forming a computing coordination group is a beginning. The MIS department can then furnish services that can keep the MIS department at the forefront of corporate computer activities. It is through this service that controls can be applied to areas that require them.

The responsibility for directing computer activity within the corporation can remain in the MIS department only if it approaches the use of alternative computer resources with a spirit of cooperation.

Reference

1. Bailey, Gade, et al. *Distributed Computing in the Early 1980's—The Environment and the Requirements.* GUIDE Secretary Distribution (GSD 50), 1977.

9 A Strategy for Systems Implementation

by David Tommela

INTRODUCTION

Many DP installations face a tremendous challenge in fulfilling their users' needs. Aspects of this challenge include:
- Demands for new, large, online systems to meet complex business needs
- Increasing backlogs of systems maintenance work
- Pressures exerted by a turbulent economy
- Increased emphasis on meeting development schedules to cope with a changing business environment

Traditional approaches to large online systems development are proving ineffective as solutions to current DP problems. These approaches typically result in the following difficulties:
- The user is forced to wait until the end of the systems development life cycle before receiving any benefits. In some instances, this delay can be years.
- Because of protracted development cycles, the application specifications to which the system is built do not meet current business needs.
- The user experiences difficulty in adapting to the new system. This difficulty is usually encountered when the "big bang" theory of implementation is employed (i.e., the old system terminates one day and the new one is operational the next).
- The backlogs for DP maintenance (correcting errors) and enhancements (revised or new functions) grow to nearly unmanageable proportions. This problem stems from the difficulties in testing an entire system, premature freezing of requirements, and discovery of needed enhancements after the system is operational.
- The credibility of the DP department is seriously damaged. The users are rightfully intolerant of long development periods and missed schedules—even if they share responsibility for these events.

This chapter focuses on a group of approaches that mitigates these problems by enabling another strategy for systems implementation. Using one approach by itself makes chances of reaping full benefits remote. Using the recommended approaches in concert and even expanding on them can significantly

improve the effectiveness of the DP department. The topics discussed in this chapter are:
- Systems development life cycle
- User participation
- Generalized system architecture
- Transition systems
- Prototypes

SYSTEMS DEVELOPMENT LIFE CYCLE

The systems development life cycle used by a DP organization helps determine the optional strategies available for implementation. Yet this factor is often overlooked when an organization seeks the causes for lengthy development times. The impact of new techniques (e.g., structured analysis) on the life cycle is also ignored when such techniques are introduced to improve the development process.

Traditional Development Life Cycles

Each DP organization has some systems development life cycle that defines the steps in developing an information system. The number of steps varies widely but generally fits into the following framework:
- Feasibility study—determining the economic and technological advisability of initiating a new development effort
- Analysis—ascertaining the functions performed by an existing automated or manual system and defining and analyzing new functions required to enhance the process
- Design—determining the software and hardware architecture of the new system and defining the logical structure and specifications of the application functions
- Construction—developing programs and testing and preparing training materials and user procedures
- Implementation—initiating activities for testing, training, and system installation; continuing maintenance and enhancement

The employment of this development life cycle usually follows the forms shown in Figures 9-1 and 9-2. These figures show the relationships of phases, not the relative durations of each phase.

Figure 9-1 depicts the serial approach, where each phase is completed before the next begins. This approach is suited to projects of short duration (less than six months) and with limited staffing (approximately three people). Typically, the applications are simple and straightforward in that the number and complexity of functions and their relationships are easily grasped by the developer. Therefore, it is easy to partition the work to be done.

Figure 9-2 illustrates the overlapping approach, in which some phases begin before the preceding phase is completed. Overlapping phases usually result in earlier delivery of systems. This approach is suited to projects of medium

SYSTEMS IMPLEMENTATION

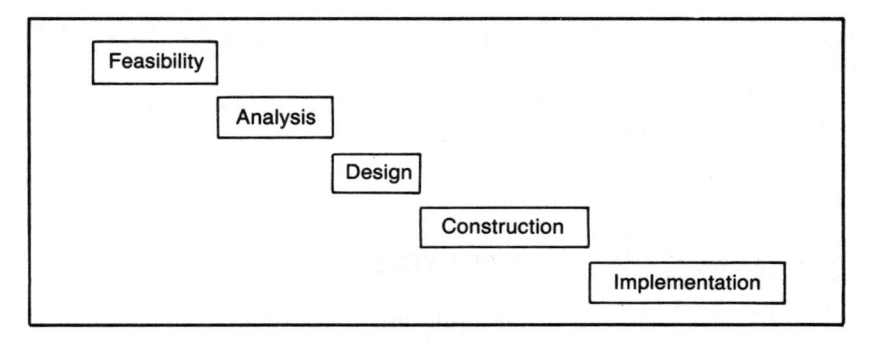

Figure 9-1. Serial Systems Development Life Cycle

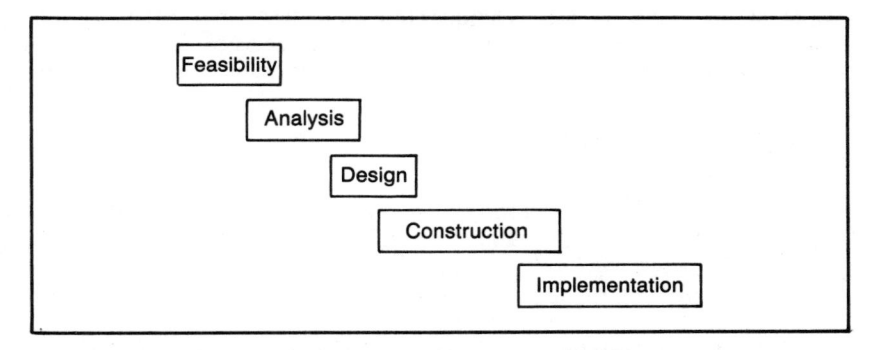

(Boxes: Feasibility → Analysis → Design → Construction → Implementation, arranged in a stepped serial sequence)

Figure 9-2. Overlapping Systems Development Life Cycle

(Boxes: Feasibility, Analysis, Design, Construction, Implementation, arranged in an overlapping stepped sequence)

duration (six to twelve months) and staffing of approximately eight people. The applications are usually more complex, and the partitioning of work assignments is more difficult because of the interrelationships of application functions.

Although these two development life cycles work well with short- and medium-length projects, certain problems inherent in both methods make them unsuitable for large, complex projects. The option to select a particular life cycle to match the task at hand is a more effective approach; however, it is usually not condoned by management.

Problems with Traditional Systems Development Life Cycles

Analyzing traditional systems development life cycles reveals the problems of applying them to a large, complex, online application.

Changing User Requirements. Users are expected to state their requirements clearly by the end of the analysis phase. The time between establishing user requirements and delivering the system can be quite lengthy. Changes to the requirements are discouraged and are often the source of dissent between DP and users. Such changes are, in fact, valuable because they reflect the user's growing knowledge of the system; however, the traditional development life cycle does not offer a means to manage such changes effectively.

Premature Decisions. This problem is a companion to changing user requirements. The user identifies requirements in a vacuum during the analysis phase. Decisions are made under the weight of a looming target date for the end of the analysis phase. Unfortunately, the user does not know enough about how the whole system will function to make these decisions. In other words, the old adage, "Users don't know what they want until they see it," is true. This serious problem manifests itself in schedule overruns and other calamities when the user sees the system.

The problem of premature decisions is compounded by two serious DP errors. First, DP may require the user to sign off or freeze the requirements. Next, DP decides which functions will be included in the system. Neither party has enough knowledge during this phase to make those decisions. Demands for certainty at the end of a development phase virtually guarantee that the system will not fully meet user needs.

Monolithic View of the System. The traditional systems development life cycle deals with the total application throughout that cycle. A large, complex application poses a formidable problem in performing such development. Even if the application is divided into comprehensible functions, the task of analyzing every function is too great. Again, the traditional systems development life cycle forces an artificial finalizing of the activities of each phase.

Big-Bang Implementation. This is the conclusion of the traditional systems development life cycle (i.e., analyze the whole problem, design a total solution, program the entire system, and implement the system). The big bang occurs when the old system stops one day and the new one starts operating the next. It is almost impossible for a user organization to cope with such an event.

Belated Problem Correction. When the user finally sees the system in operation, a torrent of change requests for enhancements pours in, in addition to the usual problem reports. The gap between user expectations and system capabilities is probably substantial. This gap is largely attributed to matching the wrong life cycle to the project. The changes must be made—often at a very substantial cost—and the lifetime cost of the new system becomes extraordinarily high.

Functional Systems Development Life Cycle

Figure 9-3 shows a third variation of the systems development life cycle. Although this approach uses the same five phases as do traditional development life cycles, deployment of the phases differs significantly. This variation is termed the functional systems development life cycle.

The source of this life cycle is structured techniques. These techniques compel the analyst to define an application hierarchically in terms of its discrete

SYSTEMS IMPLEMENTATION

Feasibility	
Base-Level Analysis	
Base-Level Design	

Subfunction A	Analysis	Design	Construction	Implementation
Subfunction B	Analysis	Design	Construction	Integration	Implementation
Subfunction C	Analysis		Design	Construction	Integration	Implementation
Subfunction D	Analysis	Design	Construction	Integration	Implementation
Subfunction E	Analysis	Design	

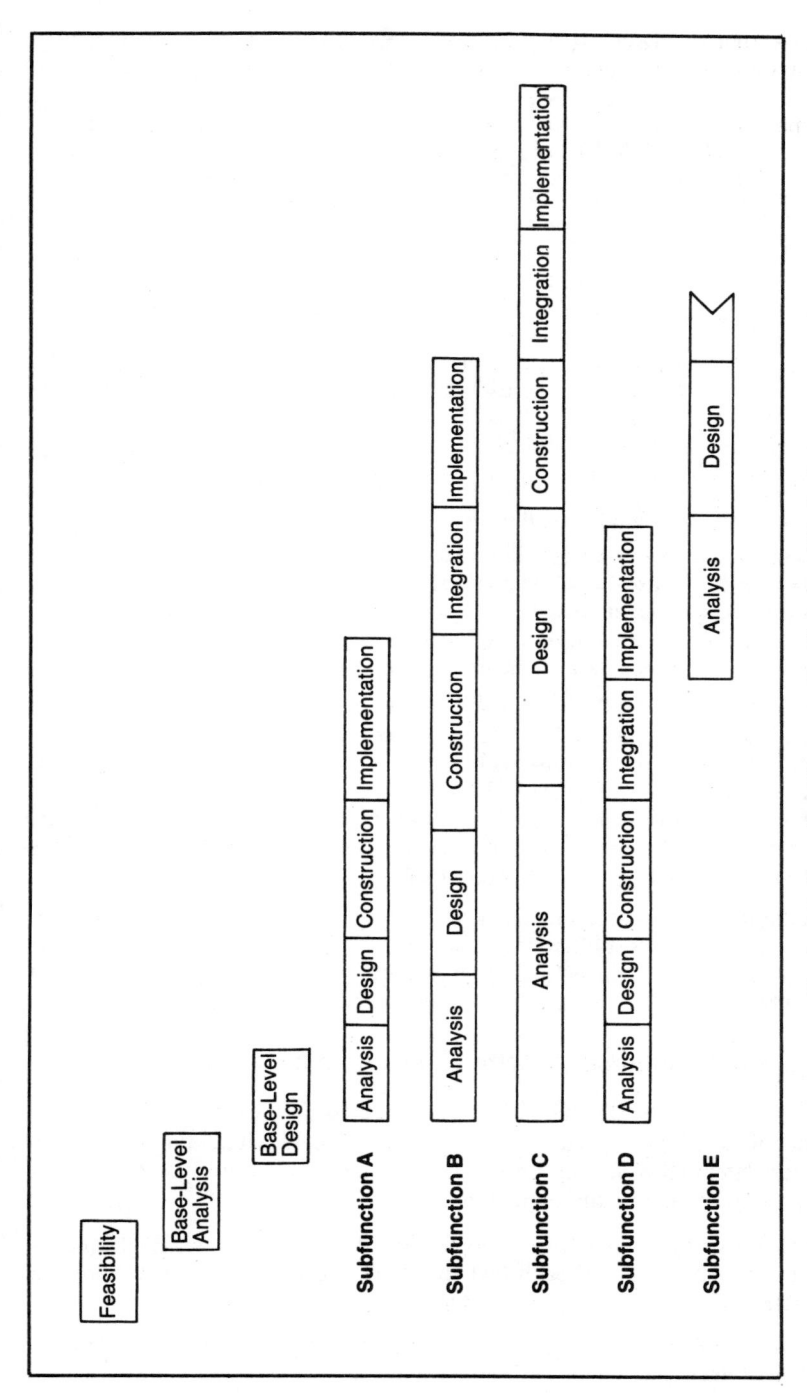

Figure 9-3. Functional Systems Development Life Cycle

functions. Analysis of these functions then leads to creation of a system design that maintains the functional orientation. Construction and implementation activities also follow this orientation.

Figure 9-4 illustrates part of the functional hierarchy of a materials system. The chart shows that the materials system consists of the six major functions identified as Level 1. All other system functions are grouped under this umbrella. Level 2 depicts the subfunctions of the major function of procurement. Level 3 is an explosion of the Level 2 subfunction of purchase orders. Level 3 components would be further segmented into one or more levels as needed. The number of levels subordinate to each subfunction (Level 2) depends upon the complexity of the subfunction.

It is apparent from a cursory glance at Figure 9-4 that describing the entire materials system in this fashion would result in hundreds of boxes on a chart. The principles of structured techniques, however, ensure that each element is grouped with its companions. Each subfunction can therefore be addressed independently, without fear of interference from another subfunction. For the most part, each subfunction can be developed and implemented individually.

Figure 9-3 shows the life cycle for such a functional development approach. The box entitled Base-Level Analysis shows that this phase begins during the feasibility study since it contributes to that study. During the base-level analysis, enough effort is expended to define the application through approximately Level 2 of the hierarchy and to ensure its integrity.

Once it appears that the top of the hierarchy is valid, the base-level design is initiated. This effort defines the basic architecture of the system and continues until the integrity of the top-level design is validated. Once the design is validated, a number of subfunctions can be developed concurrently. The number of concurrent activities depends on the amount of staffing available. Note that each subfunction then follows its own development life cycle, the duration of which depends on its complexity.

In the functional life cycle, each subfunction can be implemented independently. After the first subfunction is implemented, the other subfunctions pass through an additional development phase—integration. The system evolves as each subfunction is integrated with its predecessors.

Benefits of Functional Systems Development Life Cycle

The functional development life cycle alleviates most of the problems of the traditional development life cycle. Extensions to the functional life cycle discussed later in this chapter further diminish these problems. Specific benefits are also associated with this approach.

Early Delivery. Functions are implemented as they are developed, in contrast to the traditional approach that results in waiting until all functions are completed. The user thus has part of the system to use much earlier.

Benefit Definition. It is easier to define the benefits associated with each function of the system. This definition can even be particularized for each user

SYSTEMS IMPLEMENTATION 117

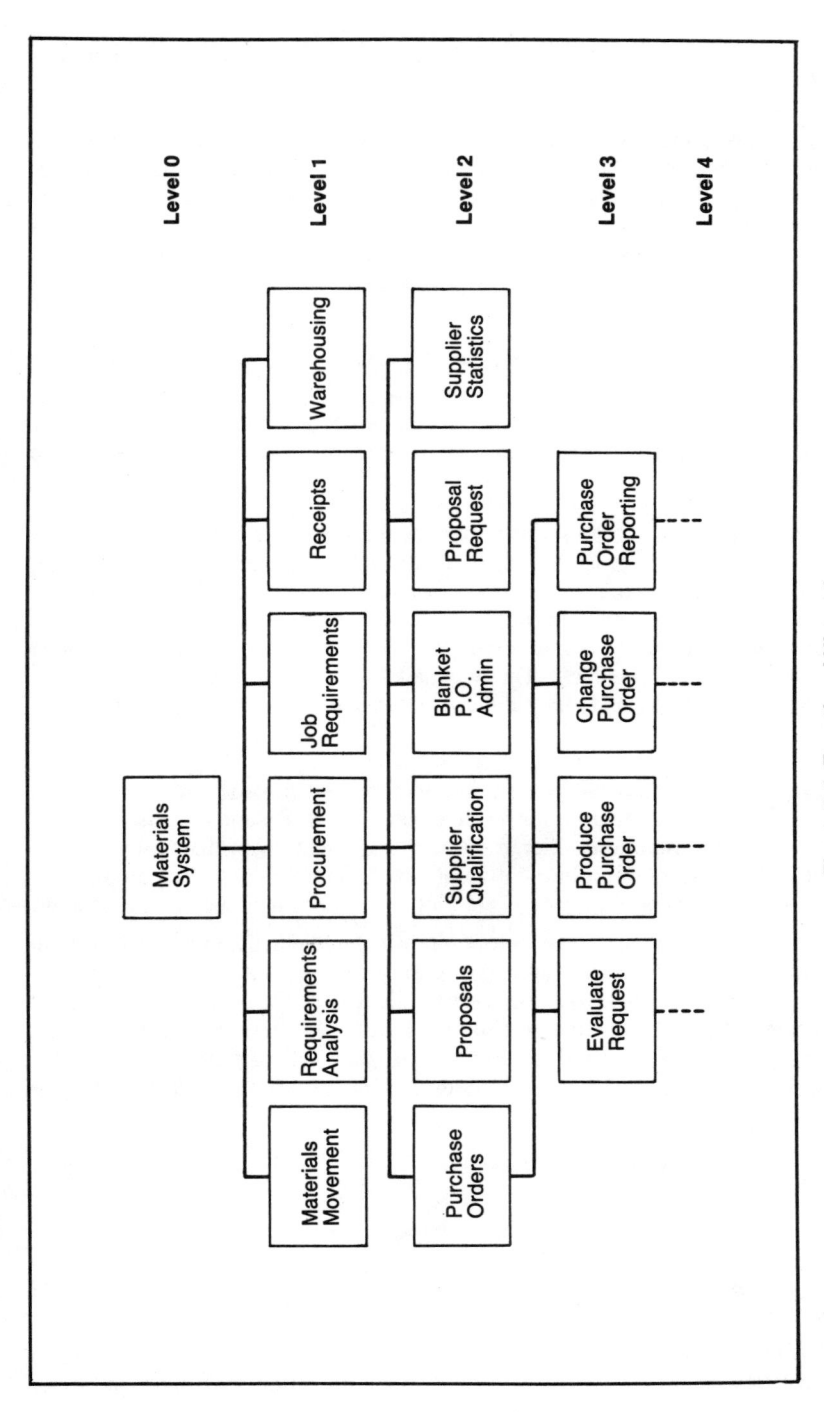

Figure 9-4. Functional Hierarchy

- Level 0: Materials System
- Level 1: Materials Movement, Requirements Analysis, Procurement, Job Requirements, Receipts, Warehousing
- Level 2: Purchase Orders, Proposals, Supplier Qualification, Blanket P.O. Admin, Proposal Request, Supplier Statistics
- Level 3: Evaluate Request, Produce Purchase Order, Change Purchase Order, Purchase Order Reporting
- Level 4: ...

of a function common to multiple users. This approach greatly facilitates validating of benefit estimates once the function is implemented.

Priority of Functions. The sequence of function development can be easily established by using benefits and external factors, such as the business climate. Obviously, the relationship of functions to one another and DP technical concerns come into play, but not to a large degree. The sequence of priorities can also change readily to meet dynamic business conditions. Setting priorities by functional benefits enables the largest percentage of benefits to be realized long before the entire system is completed.

Impact on Users. The impact on the users caused by introduction of a new system is drastically reduced when only one function is introduced at a time. The tasks of training and procedures development become more manageable. The users are able to adapt to the system more readily and can more easily cope with the change.

Impact on DP. The pressure to deliver the system is lessened. The users receive functional products rather than waiting for the entire system. Better product quality, time to measure impact on hardware resources, and improved systems developer morale are only a few of the many benefits to DP. The one negative effect must be emphasized: *It is very difficult to manage a project using the functional life cycle.* The two major sources of difficulty are multiple concurrent activities and the need for extensive communication among all personnel on the project.

System Architecture. System architecture, developed during the design phase, provides a foundation for future development. Essentially, the architecture reflects the functional hierarchy of the application in that functions are isolated from one another. Integration of new functions is easily accomplished. The integrity of the architecture is not violated as each new piece is developed.

In summary, the systems development life cycle plays an important role in determining those options available to improve the systems development process. The life cycle requires alteration to achieve fully the benefits of structured development techniques. It also should be tailored to the project. Significant advantages can be achieved by applying the concept of functional development. The functional life cycle provides a foundation for the other techniques discussed in this chapter.

USER PARTICIPATION

The approaches discussed in this chapter all emphasize early delivery of systems. DP people often lose sight of this goal in the midst of building a system. This section discusses methods for ensuring that users play a major role in systems development.

The problem usually encountered first during development of a large system is identification of the primary user of an application that spans multiple

SYSTEMS IMPLEMENTATION

departments in the corporation. The problem can exist even within one department that has multiple divisions. The solution is to select someone from a user organization as the sponsor of the system. The sponsor's job is to represent the interests of the corporation while working closely with the DP project manager. In this capacity, the sponsor has:
- Responsibility for obtaining people from user departments to work on the project
- The final decision on all application requirements
- Authority for setting development priorities
- Responsibility for representing the project to the corporation

All of these activities are done in cooperation with the project manager. In essence, the sponsor is the DP project manager's alter ego, whose primary focus is on the corporation.

Once the sponsoring organization is identified, the individual (usually a middle manager) who will act as sponsor is selected. The other users who will participate in the project are also chosen. The sponsor and users must be full-time participants, and they must be selected with utmost care. DP maintains the right to refuse a nominee as well as to replace him or her if the individual does not meet expectations. Absence of this authority seriously reduces prospects for success.

The sponsor should be a person of stature in the user organization, preferably with line, not staff, responsibilities. For the duration of the project, he or she should report to the department head. The sponsor must have authority to make decisions concerning the project. The most important attribute for a sponsor is communications skill. The other users should be selected for their expertise in the application (e.g., purchasing, warehousing). These individuals also must have authority to speak for their organizations.

The next step is assigning users to particular project teams. The teams should be organized functionally; for example, the user with expertise in purchasing should be assigned to the purchasing team. Some teams require users from several organizations to provide expertise in one function, such as warehousing. The user/DP teams are assigned to the project until completion; therefore, it is virtually mandatory that user and DP personnel share the same office space.

User Activities

The user's role is significant once the project is under way. Table 9-1 is a sample list of user activities during the project life cycle; it is by no means exhaustive.

The sponsor and several key users work with DP in conducting the feasibility study. Their primary contribution is their knowledge of the application and of its operational environment.

During the analysis phase, users have the most important role since DP has little knowledge of their jobs. The task is to obtain and document the user's knowledge; thus, the participation of users representing all application areas is

Table 9-1. User Responsibilities

Phase	Activities
Feasibility	Identifying requirements Estimating benefits
Analysis	Defining existing functions Defining new functions
Design	Defining document/screen/report formats Guiding design decisions Learning the design
Construction	Developing test data Preparing training materials Writing procedures Preparing facilities
Implementation	Testing Conducting training Monitoring implementation

critical. An ineffective way to establish user requirements is for a DP analyst to interview users and document the information. A more effective way is to ask the user to document his or her knowledge using whatever tools are employed for the task. If structured analysis techniques are used, the user should be taught how to use such tools as data flow diagrams and structured English. The DP staff can advise in the use of tools while learning about the application from the user. In this way, the user bears greater responsibility than does DP for the analysis phase of the project.

In the design phase, users advise on how requirements will be met. Users can have primary responsibility for designing I/O formats. During the analysis phase, DP learned the application; now the user learns how the system will function. User activities during the construction and implementation phases remain traditional.

In summary, user participation should be proactive throughout the systems development life cycle. This type of involvement substantially reduces many problems usually encountered by DP on a development project.

GENERALIZED SYSTEM ARCHITECTURE

There are two components of a generalized system architecture. The first is a logic structure for performing a software function; the second is the generalized software to perform the function in any application environment. Variables to make the software application-specific are provided in tables prepared by a programmer. Program code is not written.

Generalized architecture has proved to be unusually effective for online systems. Its advantages include:
- A standard interface image to the terminal user for all applications
- Reductions in development time by 50 percent or more

SYSTEMS IMPLEMENTATION   121

- A standard system architecture with proven error-free code
- One copy of the executable code
- Improved flexibility of DP staff assignment by enabling a maintenance programmer to quickly adapt to multiple applications
- Simplified documentation
- Ease of upgrading all applications with improved capabilities

A generalized architecture can be developed by any DP organization, for both online and batch functions. The process consists of:
- Designing a function for a system (e.g., inquiry to a materials file)
- Evaluating the design to determine the inquiry activities common to all applications
- Identifying activities unique to each application
- Using tables to describe unique attributes of an application
- Writing the common routines to generate the necessary tables

This approach has been successfully applied to inquiry, order entry, data validation, and order update functions for a variety of applications. Table 9-2 illustrates the differences between developing an online CICS update transaction the standard way and using a generalized architecture approach.

The example in Table 9-2 is a hypothetical update transaction containing 25 data elements. The transaction involves presenting a fill-in-the-blanks order display, accepting data, editing and validating data inputs, redisplaying edited and validated inputs, and accepting a completed update. Coding is in CICS command-level COBOL. The left column in Table 9-2 shows the number of COBOL/CICS statements needed at each stage of the transaction. The right column shows the statements and table entries required for the same transaction when a generalized architecture approach is used. The specific numbers are not important, but the difference between the two columns is significant. The difference in time required for each solution is readily apparent.

In summary, a generalized system architecture developed using the concepts of structured design plays a major role in increasing the number of implementation options. A generalized architecture has great potential for reducing development time while maintaining design integrity.

TRANSITION SYSTEMS

The preceding sections of this chapter address approaches to the systems development effort. In addition to intrinsic benefits, these approaches can also provide a foundation for implementation strategies that can lead to significant improvements in service to users. One of these strategies is the use of transition systems.

A transition system is a means of easing the conversion to the new application system. It is a temporary system developed to interface with the existing one. Both systems are replaced by the new system at a later date.

Table 9-2. Standard versus Generalized Architecture Systems Development

Standard CICS Programming

Task	COBOL Statements
Map definition with mapping support	75
Main line coding for new transaction	10
Code update transaction	1,400
Code validations and edits	1,500
Code redisplay of data for update	400
Code transaction completion routine	400
Code I/O	500
Total	4,285

Generalized Architecture Definitions

Task	COBOL Statements	Table Entries
Map definition with mapping support	75	0
Define new transaction		3
Define update attributes		6
Define validations and edits		80
Define screen data		75
Code transaction completion		100
Code I/O	500	
Totals	575	264

Reasons for Transition Systems

The transition system is designed as a stop-gap measure pending implementation of the new system. A transition system substantially reduces pressure on DP regarding schedules and enhances user/DP interfaces.

Many development efforts today replace batch with online systems; old system functions are enhanced and new functions added. The greatest opportunity for transition systems is when developing online systems, although the concept can be applied to other areas. Quite simply, a transition system involves building an online front end to an existing batch system (improving an existing function by replacing its paper input documents). The existing system continues to receive inputs in the same format, but the medium changes. It is important not to add new functions to the existing batch system because that activity conflicts with efforts to build a new system. The greatest advantage of a transition system is that some benefits become available long before the new system is completed.

If structured techniques are used to develop the new system, the appropriate time to begin transition efforts is after completing the analysis of the existing one. The products of these tasks delineate the functions of the old system. It is

SYSTEMS IMPLEMENTATION

important to maintain the functional orientation because it simplifies the later process of replacing the transition system with new system functions.

Development Method

The transition system should be developed with a generalized architecture. Processes such as screen presentation, data validation, and data access can be table driven. Such online processes as inquiry can also be generalized. Using a standard architecture reduces development time to a matter of days. Software generators such as IBM's DMS (Development Management System) can also help in this regard.

The most difficult task in building a transition system is obtaining the data validation criteria. Often this information can be obtained only by reading existing program code to ensure identification of nuances not available in documentation. The most time-consuming part of development is testing, which is exceptionally rigorous because online facilities are used.

The transition system software is discarded once the new system is developed since it is easier to write new programs than to modify old ones. In fact, industry studies show that it is more effective to rewrite a program if more than 10 percent of the code requires alteration. Maintaining a functional orientation is also important if the code is going to be considered disposable because it facilitates the replacement process.

Transition systems allow rapid development of interim solutions. These efforts need not employ the rigorous development associated with the main project. Minimum documentation and perhaps different development techniques are warranted for software with such a short life.

Benefits of Using a Transition System

The benefits of using transition systems are substantial and include:
- Time lags in submission and processing of batch documents and error corrections are eliminated. It may also be possible to reduce the data entry staff.
- The online network is established before the arrival of the new system. DP has time to gain experience with the network, facilitating the later move to the new system.
- End users become accustomed to using a terminal.
- Benefits are realized early.
- DP gains experience in building an online system for this application before designing the new system.
- The pressure on DP to accelerate development is reduced.

PROTOTYPES

The use of prototypes is another implementation strategy that can significantly improve service to users. Ideally, a prototype is used before the final system is developed; however, current software technology is insufficient to accomplish this goal. Nonetheless, a prototype can provide significant benefits even after the final system is developed.

The prototype period begins once a function has been developed and tested for either the transition system or for the new system. The software is installed as operational, but authorization to use it is restricted to one or two user organizations. For example, if an online materials function were being implemented in a retail organization, only one or two stores would use the prototype online receiving function, while the others would continue using the existing method. Using a prototype should not be confused with parallel testing. The prototype system is used on a full production basis.

Reasons for Prototypes

Even the best requirements specifications are unlikely to remain unchanged once the system is installed and operating. Unfortunately, what the users agree to on paper is often not what they actually want when they see it in real life. Online systems are particularly susceptible to this problem. An earlier section of this chapter discussed a method for assigning users to work on a project to minimize this problem. The basic reason for using a prototype is that it is easier to make changes to a system when it is not fully installed throughout the organization. The duration of a prototype depends on many factors, including application complexity, number of changes identified, and hardware limitations. Usually two to six weeks is sufficient time to evaluate the system thoroughly.

Conducting the Prototype

The project team must participate fully in the prototype, observing the training classes and assisting as needed. Staff members should sit with the terminal operators to gain an understanding of the environment in which the system is functioning. Comments, suggestions, and criticisms should be logged for later evaluation. Meetings with the terminal users should be held at the end of the day to review the items logged.

A flurry of comments is likely to arise during the first few days or weeks. Initial comments tend to be superficial and to necessitate only cosmetic changes to the prototype. Many comments originate from misunderstandings that should have been eliminated in the training classes. As users gain experience, comments become more substantive and may even reveal a need for major redesign efforts. The purpose of prototyping is to bring these questions to the surface.

Making Changes

The cardinal rule of prototyping is to make all needed changes before the system is expanded to include all users. Changes can range from the reformatting of data on a screen to the complete redevelopment of a function. It seldom

SYSTEMS IMPLEMENTATION

makes sense to provide the system to all users when it is known to be inadequate. If the concept of installing discrete functions has been followed, a total rewrite of a particular function probably will not require that much time. Adherence to this principle means that full production begins with no maintenance backlog. Furthermore, future change requests will be virtually nonexistent.

DP's rapid response to requested changes is of the utmost importance. Many minor changes can be implemented for the next day's business, for example. Rapid response gains user confidence and respect; if a change is not made promptly, the user may encounter the undesirable item hundreds of times a day while using the system. Thus, a minor problem can quickly become a significant irritant.

Each suggestion or complaint received should be thoroughly assessed from the perspective of the operating environment. Even small items like highlighting of data fields can be significant if the lighting conditions of the office environment are considered. The analysis of each suggestion or complaint should be explained in detail to the originator.

Hardware Assessment

Prototyping offers an excellent opportunity to measure the system's impact on network and computer resources. This is often overlooked and results in users who are disgruntled because response time at the terminal is 10 seconds although it was designed to be 5 seconds. The prototype should last long enough to check network management procedures for communication failures, computer failures, requests for vendor assistance, and so on. The user is affected by these matters as well, so it is best to obtain user participation.

Training Assessment

Particular attention should be paid to the adequacy of training programs. The same process used to evaluate the application should be applied to these programs because inadequacies not corrected can cause problems for a long time.

In summary, a prototype offers an exceptional opportunity to implement an error-free system tailored to user needs. Best of all, it results in users who are pleased with the development effort.

CONCLUSION

This chapter has discussed systems development concepts that can provide new strategies for system implementation. These concepts are not theoretical; they are successful in actual practice. In addition to the advantages gained by following the recommended approaches, there are some subtle effects on the overall DP operation that bear brief discussion.

Systems Auditors. Many auditors are accustomed to traditional development practices. Departure from this norm imposes additional educational burdens on DP.

Changes in User Participation. These approaches require considerable user involvement in ways perhaps unfamiliar to the user from prior DP projects. A different type of user is needed and probably in greater numbers. Employing key management and operational users on a project can remove them from career opportunities in their organizations and can cause friction between DP and those organizations.

Ending the Project. The end of a typical development project is usually discernible. An evolution project life cycle that can be adapted to changing needs is advocated here. Such projects do not have clearly defined ends; the distinction between maintenance and development is not as clear. This may raise problems in justifying, monitoring, and evaluating projects.

Maintenance. DP can more easily establish a maintenance team when project completion is easier to identify. With an evolving system, some staff targeted for development have to be retained for maintenance instead of moving to the next function. The size of this staff grows as the system itself evolves.

Hardware Capacity. The need for additional hardware capacity increases as the system evolves. Close monitoring of capacity plans is warranted.

Management. Projects that use the ideas presented in this chapter require managers capable of performing multiple tasks, with attention to detail. The difficulties of managing, however, are overshadowed by the potential for early benefits achieved by a DP/user team.

10 Selecting Software Packages

by Raymond P. Wenig

INTRODUCTION

In 30 years of computer programming, a wealth of software has been developed; a conservative estimate is that more than 20 million programs have been written. Most programs written today represent a reinterpretation of existing software to accommodate current system capabilities.

Currently, more than 30,000 software packages are commercially available. This number is growing rapidly as more systems are developed using flexible and modular design and construction techniques. This portfolio evaluates the opportunities and risks of searching for reusable software. The following questions are addressed:
- When should you investigate using existing software?
- How much effort should be devoted to the search and evaluation?
- How does this process mesh with the development life cycle?
- How much will required modifications cost?
- Who should maintain the software?

THE FACTS ABOUT USING EXISTING SOFTWARE

The supposedly mysterious and artistic content of computer programs makes the idea of using existing software seem unnatural—akin to stealing a creation. Because systems development cost and risk factors have been escalating, however, the creative approach to systems development may be pricing itself out of the market.

There are several ways to handle this situation other than using existing software. For example, a given project could be deferred; a simple, unsophisticated approach could be taken; or a turnkey vendor (who will use existing software) or a fixed-priced, low-bid contractor (who will probably use existing software modules) could be employed.

The consideration of existing software has been increasingly accepted in many nonapplication areas (e.g., operating systems, data base managers, sorts, and terminal monitors). The increasing popularity of turnkey minicomputer systems and the development of sophisticated software packages for such applications as accounting, personnel, and payroll also have contributed to this trend.

The use of available software allows concentration of resources on improvement of the software product. It can also shorten the product delivery cycle.

When to Consider Software Reuse

Unfortunately, software does not exist for all applications, nor does every package run on every hardware configuration. It would be futile, for instance, to search for a system for inventory control of a propagating earthworm colony. On the other hand, a search for a minicomputer-based payroll system will probably uncover from 150 to 200 candidate packages. As a rule of thumb, the more common the application area, the more likely that usable software is available.

Table 10-1 provides estimates of available software packages in several application areas. These estimates have been generated by reviewing several software directories. It should be noted that when many packages are available, the probability of finding a suitable package is greater; however, it also requires more effort to select the best one. When only a few packages are available, it is easier to review them, but there may not be any that could be modified to satisfy particular functional requirements.

Table 10-1. Available Software by Application

Application Category	Estimated Number of Packages Available
Inventory Control	150
Payroll/Personnel	300
Order Entry	80
Accounts Receivable	220
Job Costing	20
Project Management	35
Text Editing	15
Statistical Analysis	40
Maintenance Management	5
Sales Analysis	60
Report Writers	20
Broadcasting Control	5
Vending Machine Control	3
Hardware Performance Analysis	10

How to Locate Reusable Software

As the volume of available software expands, it becomes more difficult to identify and locate suitable packages. Some sources to investigate include:
- Hardware vendors
- Software developers
- Turnkey companies

SELECTING PACKAGES   129

Type of Listing Source	Example/Contact	Cost	Type of Software	Remarks
Vendor Software Lists	Most major equipment makers (e.g., IBM, Burroughs, NCR)	Free	Special vendor packages Field-developed systems	Lists only programs for vendor systems Irregularly updated
Vendor Referral Directories	Several minicomputer vendors (e.g., Digital Equipment, DG, Datapoint)	Free	Programs produced by contracted OEM vendors Usually applications oriented	No quality guidelines Irregularly updated
User Group Libraries	Most computer vendors (e.g., IBM-SHARE, DECUS)	$5–$500 membership fee	Variety Mostly subroutines and utilities Few applications	Standardized abstracts Irregularly updated
Published Directories	*ICP Directories* *AUERBACH Applications Software Reports* *Minicomputer Software Quarterly*	$65–$350 subscription (usually 1 year)	Mostly applications	Regularly updated Many cross-reference indexes
Trade Associations	National Association of State Information Systems Office Products Auto Parts	Varies	Trade applications	Not updated Variable content and quality
Government-Supported Agencies	COSMIC—University of Georgia Federal Software Exchange	$0–$75	Wide range of government-sponsored software products. Technical and commercial applications	Detailed listings Irregularly updated
Technical Press Advertising	*Computerworld* *Datamation*	$0–$25/year subscription	Proprietary systems from software vendors	Variable content No indexes
Search Publications	Computer Hotline User Groups	$0–$50/year membership	Requests for specific software sources Listings of new offerings	Regular publication No indexes Repeated requests

Figure 10-1. Software Location Chart

- Users
- Hobbyists
- Government agencies
- Trade associations
- Universities
- Cooperative libraries

Unfortunately, the offerings of these sources are not cataloged and listed in a common directory. Reusable software is listed (somewhat haphazardly) in several sources; Figure 10-1 shows the primary sources for locating reusable software.

The number of sources for information on available software has been increasing. New publications appear from time to time, more user groups (e.g., The Association of Minicomputer Users) are organizing software information and/or trading bureaus, and more commercial space is being used to advertise available software.

It should be pointed out, however, that all of these sources do not list all available software. Many firms with reusable software feel that they are not in the software business; thus, they do not bother to list their systems in directories. If contacted, however, many of these firms would consider selling their systems to appropriate buyers.

ASSESSMENT OF RISK FACTORS

As mentioned earlier, using available software is not without risk. The positive side of the balance includes opportunity, time, cost, and proven systems. The risk factors include:
- Search time and costs
- Impossibility of modifying functional requirements
- Program modification costs
- Unique construction details
- Poor documentation
- Lack of maintainability
- Hardware configuration variances
- Minimal or nonexistent support
- Inefficient throughput
- Growth limits
- Unknown (latent) bugs

The major risks associated with software acquisition and reuse are summarized in Figure 10-2.

To some extent, considering the reuse of software is like shopping for a used car. A buyer can shop for make, model, color, and price and then test drive a car but can only accurately evaluate the car after using it for a period of time. With software, it may be more difficult to satisfy the buyer's requirements because more of the operational aspects of the product are hidden. In addition, as a rule, software products require customizing.

SELECTING PACKAGES 131

Element of Risk	Potential Impact	Control Methods	Options
Search Time and Effort	Wasted if no usable product is found	Set fixed limits on search project	Use a consultant with specialized expertise Limit the search
Finding Software that Answers only Some of the Requirements	Costly modification An unacceptable final system	Keep the requirements general Define the requirements and desirable features separately	Build the system in-house Estimate modification costs early
Difficulty with Modification	Costly modification and maintenance	Detailed review of software structures, content, and design	Use package as is Avoid the product Treat as a temporary solution
Lack of Support	Costly internal maintenance	Buy support Training commitment	Use package as is Build internal support source
Inefficient Product	Costly operation	Throughput reviews Operational evaluation	Revise product to make it more efficient Absorb the cost
Limits Growth	Required modification Shortened useful life of the product	Evaluate the limitations Develop expansion design	Avoid the product Treat as a temporary solution
Unknown Bugs	System failures Costly repairs	Critical/detailed evaluation of the product	Contractual warranty Support team
Sloppy Construction	Difficult to modify/maintain	Detailed evaluation	Avoid the product Contractual clean-up Internal clean-up Use package as is
Poor Documentation	Difficult to learn and maintain the system Unanticipated costs	Critical review of documentation	Rewrite the system as a learning expense Avoid the product
Hardware Configuration Variances	Modification required to assure operation on user equipment	Design evaluation	Contractual arrangement with a package vendor Internal learning process
Does not Satisfy User Needs	Major modification required Ill feeling toward the DP department	User evaluation and commitment	Avoid the product Plan major modification
Unstable Vendor	Support problems	Acquire source rights	Avoid the product Plan in-house support

Figure 10-2. Risk Chart

PACKAGE EVALUATION

The major evaluation criteria for software packages are outlined in Figure 10-3. A thorough evaluation reduces the risk that a given package will not meet the organization's needs.

Factor	Specifics	Evaluation Techniques
History of the Product	Knowledge of the product's development and evolution	Builder reviews, documentation updates, and interviews
Construction	Structure and flexibility	Detailed walkthrough of the product
Operation	Flow, control, and throughput	Observation, inspection, and testing
Utilization	Quality and usefulness of the output and satisfaction of the users	Interviews, tests, and questioning of other users
Adaptability	Satisfactory adjustment to new users	Interviewing of other users Developing a detailed conversion/adoption plan
Ease of Modification	Cost of required modification Critical to the acceptance and use of the product	Design plan and modification analysis Trial modification of the product
Maintenance	Continued operation and adjustment of the product to user requirements	Questioning of other users Internal support planning

Figure 10-3. Evaluation Criteria

The Modification Dilemma

Software packages seldom (if ever) match user requirements exactly. Consequently, the systems must be modified (modifying the modus operandi of the user department to fit the software package is not suggested). Note, however, that the cost of modification often exceeds the cost of acquiring the software.

The modification dilemma is that software packages must be modified to meet the needs of the users, but the required modifications are more risky and difficult to design and build than a new system. The acquired package has certain limitations and idiosyncrasies; modifications must be constructed around them. Unfortunately, these limitations and idiosyncrasies are often neither obvious nor well documented.

HANDLING THE RISK

The decision to purchase a software package must be based on the cost of acquisition plus the cost of required modification adjusted by the risk of the sucessful implementation of the modification. Although acquisition cost can be carefully estimated, the cost of modification should include sizable contingency value to compensate for unknown and unpredictable difficulties.

SELECTING PACKAGES

Modifying a software package requires a clear set of user requirements with the areas of necessary modification defined with reference to the package being considered. Users should, of course, be involved in this process. The evaluation team and/or the product vendor should then be able to develop a list of changes needed to meet the requirements statement.

The next step is to determine who will make the changes, at what cost, under what conditions, and over how long a period of time. Here again there are several alternatives; the primary choices are outlined in Figure 10-4.

There are other ways to circumvent the modification problem. It is often possible, for instance, to use the package as is by developing a series of interface modules to produce the desired results. Another approach is to extract the major elements from the software package and build routines to perform the required functions. Regardless of the approach used, it is imperative to weigh the risk of making the modification.

It is recommended that early in the review process a preliminary estimate of the complexity of the required modification be made. This should be used to compare available packages and as a basis for calculating more detailed work and cost estimates.

OPERATIONAL CONSIDERATIONS

The way in which a reusable software package operates is a major consideration because the system must be compatible with the user's organization, equipment, and procedures. The operational considerations for software packages are summarized in Figure 10-5.

Operational considerations can affect the processes of learning, supporting, and working with a purchased system. Inefficient operation can result in excessive cost, a short system life, and user frustration and dissatisfaction with the package.

DEVELOPMENT LIFE CYCLE FOR SOFTWARE REUSE

The consideration of reusable software packages requires some adjustment in the usual development life cycle. The adjusted life cycle is shown in Figure 10-6.

The development life cycle is most affected by software acquisition in the design phase, which is expanded to include the software search, evaluation, acquisition, and modification. If any of these steps fails to produce an acceptable candidate package, however, the usual development life cycle can be reinstituted to pursue in-house design of the system.

CONCLUSION

The reuse of existing software is becoming more and more practical because of the expanding number of available systems, the use of smaller, more functionally constrained minicomputer systems, and the quality of structured

Source	Approach	Advantages	Disadvantages
Software Creator	Extra-cost contract for modification	Knowledge of the system Lowest cost Possible fixed price	Lack of user control Possible incorrect interpretation of requirements
Internal Programmers	Internal design, development, and installation of the required modification	Knowledge of the user(s) Knowledge of system requirements Learning the system is useful for future required changes.	Lack of knowledge of the system Cost of learning the system Domino errors
Third-Party Software Vendor	Review, estimate, and contract for the required modification.	Outside resources Explicit commitment	Cost of learning the software and the application Lack of control Maintenance
Other Users	Locate another user who has made similar modifications	Saves time and money Other users may have solved many of the system's problems.	May be unable to identify the appropriate change(s) Maintenance Competitive aspect

Figure 10-4. Alternative Sources of Software Modification

Operational Characteristic	Potential Benefits	Preferred Alternatives
Use of Standards	Maintainability Flexibility to change	Defined standards Logical conventions Documentation of the explanations
Error Handling	Accuracy of processing	Clearly defined edits Demonstration error edits
Operations Documentation	Learning speed Flexibility of use	Comprehensive documentation Good operator messages from the system
Support	Continued use and dependence on the product	Vendor supplied (for a fee) Internal commitment
Access to Future Changes	Inexpensive growth of the system	Sharing by users Cost sharing new developments
Recovery Capabilities	Control of failures	Flexible recovery routines Good audit trails
Systems Documentation	Modification and learning of the system	Comprehensive set Embedded code documentation
Source-Code Rights	Freedom to modify the system Independence from the vendor	Open access Escrowed protection
User Groups	Sharing of ideas and problems	User cooperation

Figure 10-5. Operational Factors

SELECTING PACKAGES 135

Phase	Activity	Time Range	Pitfalls
Define Requirements	Specify required and desirable features.	2 weeks to several months	Incomplete specifications Not separating requirements from desirable features
Search for Suitable Packages	Match program requirements to available packages.	1–4 weeks	Finding no matches Insufficient information
Package Evaluation	Review and evaluate software packages for match to requirements.	2–6 weeks	Learning package details
Software Acquisition	Negotiate and contract for acceptable software packages.	1–4 weeks	Lack of agreement Compromises
Modification Planning and Design	Detail the required modifications.	2–8 weeks	Difficulty in defining the required modifications Inadequate documentation
Modification and Testing	Build and test the modifications.	Varies	Inadequate test data Modifications that do not work Inefficient modifications
Implementation	Install and cut-over to the modified system.	2–6 weeks	Misinterpretation of the requirements Operational flaws
Performance Review	Evaluate the system, and plan future modifications and enhancements.	4 days to 2 weeks	Inappropriate expectations System or modification flaws

Figure 10-6. Modified Development Life Cycle for Software Evaluation, Purchase, Modification, and Reuse

systems. It may be worth a short evaluation effort at the beginning of each development project to determine whether a suitable software package is available.

If candidate packages are found, a detailed evaluation should be conducted. Even if the available software is found to be inappropriate, the reviewers will have gained some knowledge on approaches to the application area as well as ideas for design.

It is also possible that a software package might be acquired as a temporary system while a tailored system is being designed and built. Such an approach can save time, provide the user with an interim solution, and give the designers a learning model from which to build.

11 Structured Techniques

by Pat Duran
and Al McCready

INTRODUCTION

Structured techniques evolved as an attempt to solve specific technical and applications problems. Applications have become increasingly complex, and the tools that were useful for developing a straightforward reporting application, for example, may not be adequate for defining the software to support a nationwide sales and order processing system.

As the proliferation of software packages indicates, most simple software problems have been solved. Many DP managers today expend more effort controlling the acquisition of software than overseeing its development; they need tools that will help them to understand their own requirements and to evaluate how well different packages satisfy those requirements. DP managers who still manage software development are tackling applications of increasing complexity, some of which have never successfully been done before; such managers need tools to help control these massive development efforts.

Structured Programming

In the sixties, when structured programming was being discussed and developed in academic circles, the emphasis was on hardware rather than software. This explains the lack of response to the early work on structured programming [1, 2].

The *New York Times* project of 1971 is generally recognized as the first well-documented demonstration that structured programming could pay off in a production environment [3, 4]. The project utilized both top-down structured programming and the chief programmer team concept. The results of this project are significant because noticeably improved programmer productivity and greater system reliability were achieved.

In the early seventies structured programming began to receive widespread attention from industry. The rising cost of software prompted managers to investigate ways of reducing software costs, especially the labor cost of software development and maintenance [5]. Most programs were difficult to read, understand, and maintain. Programmers developed their own styles so that even those using the same programming language had trouble understanding one another's code.

Structured programming techniques emphasized that code should be readable, understandable, and maintainable. They accomplished this by limiting the ways of stating logic and stressing the use of meaningful names and style guidelines within an organization.

Structured Design

Although structured programming worked well when applied to small programs, the results were less satisfactory on large programs or systems. Some programmers put their code through such contortions to avoid using the GOTO statement that while the resulting program contained only the three basic constructs of structured programming (sequence, selection, and iteration), it was still difficult to read. The problem was that these programs lacked an overall structure. That structure was supplied by structured design.

The seminal article on structured design appeared in 1974, and the ideas were included in IBM's courses on programmer productivity techniques [6]. These ideas were refined by Myers, Page-Jones, and Yourdon and Constantine [7, 8, 9]. Structured design emphasized improving the maintainability of systems by constructing them of loosely connected components. The idea started to gain acceptance in the mid-1970s, and education became readily available from a number of sources.

Structured design and structured programming helped solve many of the technical problems of software development. Systems that were flexible and responsive to user changes were developed within budget and on schedule, with little or no sacrifice in machine costs.

Structured Analysis

Although these technical problems were reduced by structured design and programming techniques, the problem of communications between user and system developer was not addressed. The late seventies saw an increasing interest in structured analysis that emphasized understanding and communicating of user requirements for automated support of user business activities.

Similar methods of structured analysis evolved in two ways. Most methods capitalized on certain structured design concepts [10, 11, 12]. These concepts were enhanced for use in the analysis phase and combined with data analysis and specification tools. Communications heuristics were then applied to the use of all of these tools.

The Structured Analysis and Design Technique (SADT ™) was developed in the late sixties and early seventies in response to the problems associated with defining systems requirements [13]. SADT is a tool for solving a variety of

™ SADT is a trademark of SofTech Inc.

complex problems and has been used to analyze software requirements since the early seventies.

REASONS FOR STRUCTURED TECHNIQUES

There are several reasons for employing structured techniques: the cost trends of hardware and software, software maintenance costs, rising labor costs, the ability to solve more difficult problems, and improved software quality.

Cost Trends of Hardware and Software. One reason for using structured techniques is the cost trends for hardware and software. Hardware is now cost-justifiable in a much broader range of situations and applications. This applies in circumstances where significantly increased hardware capacity can be acquired with no increase of cost and in circumstances where a particular hardware capability was not previously cost-justified.

While hardware costs now account for a decreasing percentage of the costs of creating and operating an application system, software costs have increased because the cost of labor in systems development has been rising substantially. A shortage of qualified systems development personnel has raised even further the human resource costs in systems development.

Cost of Software Maintenance. Another important justification for the implementation and development of structured techniques is the cost of software maintenance. For many years, systems were developed and implemented with little or no consideration given to maintenance costs over the life of the system. When it was recognized that systems maintenance represented approximately two-thirds of the programming and analysis resource costs over the useful life of the system, it became clear that designing and implementing a system that is relatively inexpensive to maintain could result in substantial savings. Solving this problem has been a major concern in the development of structured techniques.

Satisfying User Needs. Another concern in the development of structured techniques has been to avoid developing and implementing systems that do not satisfy user requirements. Until users can define their requirements and implement appropriate software application solutions on their own, DP professionals will be required to assist in translating requirements into functioning application systems. Structured systems analysis and design techniques are tools to assist DP professionals and knowledgeable users in creating a product that satisfies user needs.

Solving More Difficult Problems. Most of the straightforward accounting and inventory control problems have now been solved, and the solutions are available as standardized software packages. The industry is now turning toward more complex problems. Users now want DP to integrate small systems developed in the past and to develop new systems that encompass substantially broader and more complex requirements.

For example, in the past, a public utility company was content with an automated accounting system, an automated inventory system, and perhaps some automated support for the engineering staff. Today this company wants an online construction estimating system that includes materials issue, work order tracking, work order closing, and distribution of labor and materials expense to accounting. This system crosses all traditional departmental and automated system boundaries; the traditional systems analysis and design techniques and approaches, therefore, may be inadequate for producing high-quality work.

Improved Software Quality. One of the significant benefits of the implementation and use of structured techniques relates directly to the reasons for using them. (Several other benefits of using structured techniques are discussed later in this chapter.) When tools and techniques that are well suited to the organization and the situation are chosen, the quality of the product generated by the analysis, design, and implementation activities is noticeably improved. Producing a better system that is easy to maintain, flexible, more satisfying to users, and better documented is the strongest reason for using structured techniques.

CHANGES IN SOFTWARE LIFE CYCLE

The most significant change in the systems development segment of the software life cycle that results from the use of structured techniques is the increased effort expended in the early phases. This was borne out in the University of Toronto's experience in implementing structured techniques. The system developers there experienced a change in the time devoted to each phase of the life cycle. Structured design reduced the time devoted to coding and testing; structured analysis reduced the time devoted to design [14]. This shift is a natural and important part of the transition to a structured environment, where additional resources are expended in the early phases in the expectation that fewer resources will be required for the total life cycle.

Emphasis on Analysis and Design. The evolution of structured methods in systems development has caused new emphasis to be placed on the analysis and design phases. Projects can go wrong at many different points. Spending a great deal of time, energy, and money on systems maintenance indicates failures in design; extensive debugging suggests problems in module design and in coding and testing methods. Failures in the analysis phase, however, may require much more substantial rework efforts and expenditures, and attempts to recover from analysis failures often prove unsatisfactory.

Proponents of structured techniques, therefore, generally stress the importance of the analysis and design phases. In the past, the output from system testing was often the first tangible product the user could understand and evaluate. This first sample output was offered for user review and approval

STRUCTURED TECHNIQUES 141

much too late, since the system had already been designed and coded. Structured systems analysis and design techniques place user review and approval in the early phases of the project. The products of test runs are merely checked for conformance to specifications that were produced and approved much earlier in the development cycle. Changing a mock-up of a proposed report or a description of the proposed logical flow of information is less expensive, less frustrating, faster, and easier than redoing the program code and documentation.

Increased Human Resources. Because of the emphasis on the analysis and design phases of the software life cycle, management must invest more human resources in the development of a system before any program code is produced. The code produced can be expected to be better (and the time in testing shorter) because the code is written from a well-thought-out design specification.

Top-Down Approach. Another aspect of the emphasis on analysis and design is the requirement that the "big picture" be considered before details are developed. This top-down approach is an important part of structured techniques. Often there is a tendency to become immersed too quickly in the details of computer systems design without duly considering the larger structure into which the details fit. The emphasis on a top-down approach in structured techniques requires defining the higher-level system first. Increasing levels of detail can then be placed into this framework.

Constructing a Logical Model. The opportunity to build a logical model of the system before physical design and implementation begins is another advantage of structured techniques. The logical model should be a description of the system that is independent of any current or planned physical implementation. Using tools provided by various structured techniques, the logical design can be laid out in a form easily comprehended by nontechnical users. Flaws in the design that were not apparent to DP personnel can be pointed out and corrected by users, who have a greater familiarity with the working environment. Logical models enable easier user understanding and evaluation of the system design early in the development process.

Performing Activities Concurrently

The clearer definition of the system that results from structured analysis and design makes it possible to perform more activities concurrently. For example, if system outputs are clearly defined and accepted by the user department in the analysis and design phases, work can begin immediately on the development of user manuals.

Such concurrent activities are not feasible when the programmer who codes the system also makes systems design decisions. When a user manual is written concurrently with the detailed design and coding in a nonstructured environment, some of the programmer's design decisions can cause inaccuracies in the user documentation.

The opportunity for performing concurrent activities in the structured environment includes producing of detailed programming specifications and program code. If structured tools and techniques are used to produce complete, accurate, and user-approved analysis and design documents, the project manager has substantially greater freedom and flexibility in subsequent design and implementation activities.

Greater Flexibility

Because concurrent activities are possible, there is greater flexibility in delaying or postponing certain activities. For example, a hierarchical or top-down design may include modules that need not be programmed or implemented until long after certain other modules are operational. In the structured environment, this option can be chosen deliberately, rather than because of fear that problems or design flaws might make the full system too difficult to implement. Because the developers have a clear understanding of the overall system, this flexibility can be exercised, with confidence that the logical interrelationships have been defined and considered.

BENEFITS OF STRUCTURED TECHNIQUES

This section describes those benefits of structured techniques that are frequently cited by practitioners.

Increased Productivity

Structured techniques can result in as much as a 20 percent improvement in overall productivity. The bank that reported this increase used tested active statements per active person-day as the unit of measure [15]. A university division found itself "producing more procedures at a lower cost." [14] Productivity was measured in number of systems produced and enhanced rather than in lines of code, since fewer statements were used because of minimized redundancy. As these two studies show, it is difficult to compare productivity in different organizations since different measurements are used.

Quality

A number of factors can be used to judge the quality of a system; for example, number of errors found, amount of downtime, and number of user-requested changes that are not the result of business change can be used. Structured techniques are producing a change in the attitude of systems developers who are approaching the attitude of two hardware developers who, when asked to explain the success of their one software product (which had run for two years without an error), replied that they "didn't know bugs were allowed." Structured techniques are bringing people to expect error-free systems.

STRUCTURED TECHNIQUES 143

Testing thus can be seen in a different light. From the time the first diagram is drawn with structured analysis, the analyst's understanding of the user requirements is tested and improved through ongoing iterative review procedures. Testing and quality assurance are built into every step of the process.

Easier Maintenance

Maintainability is one of the primary goals of structured techniques. The quality criteria of structured design are geared to produce a design that is flexible and easy to change, with minimal disruption. Structured programming complements this by increasing the readability and understandability of the code. The post-implementation maintenance that often results from users' increased understanding of their system is minimized through the use of structured analysis, which gives users paper models of their system to experiment with, well before the system is finalized.

Improved documentation is another benefit of using structured techniques that facilitates maintenance. (Often the very existence of documentation is an improvement.) With structured techniques, the development models become the documentation so that documentation is created during development rather than after.

One bank found that structured techniques reduced the ratio of maintenance to development from 80:20 to 40:60 over a three-year period [16].

Insurance against Turnover

Structured techniques also provide insurance against personnel turnover. The expected improvement in documentation facilitates the introduction of people to a project. Rather than learn about a system by reading code or system flowcharts, they can look at diagrams that present the system in an orderly, top-down fashion. They can see the general outline of the system before analyzing the more detailed levels. The diagrams can easily be followed to focus on particular areas. This smoother orientation process is possible regardless of the stage in which the person is introduced to the project.

A team approach is another safeguard against personnel turnover. There are many variations of the team approach, but all require that several people contribute to systems development and quality assurance. The team approach provides ongoing review (using walk-throughs, the author/reader cycle, or inspections) of the system as it is being developed. Thus, a number of people become familiar with the system and are better equipped to play different roles in the development process, if necessary.

Attracting and Retaining Quality People

The best DP professionals usually want to use state-of-the-art tools and techniques; thus, a company that uses structured techniques often has a better chance of attracting people who are quality oriented. One bank considered the ability to attract and keep good people a major reason for converting to structured techniques. As Page-Jones states:

> A manager owes it to his subordinates to provide them with the most modern and most apt tools for their job. If he doesn't provide such tools, then he should not be surprised if his people become unhappy or tend to move on to other positions [8].

Attracting and educating good people is not enough to stop turnover, however. People skilled in structured techniques are more attractive to other organizations. To keep these people, opportunities for them to use their skills in a rewarding way should be provided. A progressive environment that stresses personal development will contribute to high staff morale [14].

Project Management Benefits

Some of the benefits of structured techniques are particularly applicable to the project management process itself. They include easier estimating, better project control, and increased flexibility.

Easier Estimating. Most estimating techinques require dividing the projects into smaller units. Since partitioning into successively smaller units is an essential aspect of the structured techniques, they provide a natural application-related breakdown to serve as the basis for estimating. For example, a structured design depicts a system as a hierarchy of modules with clearly defined interfaces. Programming and integration efforts can be estimated for each module and for the whole system. Similarly, the products of analysis (which are also partitioned into small units) can be used to estimate the design effort required.

Although this method of estimating projects is not uncommon, estimates done in a structured environment are unusually reliable. This accuracy results primarily from the clarity and completeness of the early stages of the analysis and design.

Attempts are currently underway to develop metrics that will facilitate programming and design estimates. The method is based on the number of components in the products of structured design and structured analysis. Until these metrics are further developed, estimates will still be largely subjective, based on individual experience with similar projects. Structured techniques, however, provide a more concrete framework for these estimates. In addition, tracking actual versus estimated performance on projects and tailoring the next set of estimates accordingly will help to reduce the subjective nature of estimating.

Better Project Control. Because estimates can be based on discrete components, project plans can be developed on the same foundation. This greatly aids project monitoring and control. Rather than monitoring by major milestones, it is possible to monitor by "inch-pebbles" [9]. Slippages, therefore,

STRUCTURED TECHNIQUES 145

are noticed sooner, when there is a better chance of successful corrective action (or, at the very least, an opportunity to revise estimates accordingly.)

Top-down incremental implementation also allows progress to be measured in terms of the number of working modules rather than in number of lines or modules coded. Integration testing starts as soon as there are two modules, and the most important interfaces are tested first. When the programming is 90 percent complete in this environment, it can truly mean that 90 percent of the modules are working rather than that the programmers think they have found 90 percent of the bugs in the code. (The last 10 percent often takes longer to correct than the first 90 percent.)

The review procedures of structured techniques also aid in project monitoring since they increase the visibility of the developing product. For example, the author/reader cycle of SADT is particularly useful in tracking progress and identifying bottlenecks that require management attention. The peer review or walkthrough techniques offered by structured methods provide a quality-assurance function not readily obtainable before.

Increased Flexibility for Managers. Structured techniques increase management flexibility in two main areas:
- The development process itself
- Personnel assignment

The previous section on changes in the software life cycle discussed the flexibility allowed by the overlapping of development activities. A related benefit of structured techniques is the ability to implement systems in several versions of increasing sophistication rather than as a whole. This approach offers the following specific benefits:
- Gives the user a product sooner. The first version should address the most pressing user needs and also afford user personnel the opportunity to learn new procedures gradually.
- Increases morale because the system can be seen up and running.
- Decreases the cost of user-requested changes that result from using the system, since supplementary versions have not yet been coded.
- May result in reducing the size of the system (and thereby the cost) if a user decides that the details of the last version are unnecessary.

The combination of structured design and top-down implementation techniques enables gradual implementation. The number of versions and the content of each are decided by the user and the system developers.

Another area of increased flexibility for managers is personnel assignment. Since in both structured analysis and structured design the new system is subdivided in such a way that the interfaces among the components are minimized, the design and/or programming of those components can be assigned to different people, with assurance that the pieces will fit together. Analysts can even divide the analysis work once a high-level partitioning is accepted. Of course, structured techniques do not make it possible to assign 100 people to a 100-person-month project and ensure its completion in one month [15]. More work can be done independently and simultaneously, however.

User Satisfaction

It is important to remember that systems are developed to serve some business function. In the final analysis, the user can best assess how well the system meets that goal. Perhaps the single most important benefit of structured techniques is increased user satisfaction. The user has increased confidence in the system because it performs as specified. Bugs can be corrected in a timely fashion. Easier maintenance means that the system keeps pace with the user's changing business needs. Better management control of the development process means that the user can be better informed of project status. Gradual implementation gives the user a system sooner, facilitating training and correction of misunderstandings.

User satisfaction is increased by user involvement in the development process. Structured analysis, in particular, requires almost constant dialogue between user and analyst—the analyst produces a graphic model of the system, and the user reviews it at every step. Misunderstandings are corrected early, and the user can be assured that the project is always directed at the right target. Many users find the structured analysis models themselves very helpful, and some users are now finding it useful to incorporate these models into their training for new employees.

CONCLUSION

Structured techniques work well, but the most important factor in a project's success is still the quality of the people doing the work. Structured techniques will not transform a noncommunicative, detail-oriented person into an analyst capable of seeing the big picture and communicating it to the user and the designer. In the hands of a skilled practitioner—or even a novice with good natural abilities—structured techniques can achieve dramatic improvements in the systems development effort.

References

1. Dijkstra, E.W. "Programming Considered as a Human Activity." *Proceedings of the IFIP Congress*, New York NY, 1965.
2. Bohm, C. and Jacopini, G. "Flow Diagrams, Timing Machines, and Languages with only Two Formation Rules." *Communications of the ACM*, Vol. 9, No. 5 (May 1966), 366–371.
3. Baker, F. Terry. "Chief Programmer Team Management of Production Programming." *IBM Systems Journal*, Vol. 11, No. 1 (1972), 56–73.
4. Baker, F. Terry. "System Quality Through Structured Programming." *AFIPS Proceedings 1972 Fall Joint Computer Conference*, 1972.
5. Boehm, B.W. "Software and its Impact: A Quantitative Assessment." *Datamation*, Vol. 18, No. 5 (May 1973), 48–59.
6. Stevens, W.P., Myers, G.J., and Constantine, L.L. "Structured Design." *IBM Systems Journal*, Vol. 13, No. 2 (1974).
7. Myers, G. *Reliable Software through Composite Design*. New York: Van Nostrand Reinhold Co, 1975.
8. Page-Jones, M. *The Practical Guide to Structured Systems Design*. New York: Yourdon Press, 1980.
9. Yourdon, E. and Constantine, L. *Structured Design*. New York: Yourdon Press, 1975.
10. DeMarco, T. *Structured Analysis and Systems Specification*. New York: Yourdon Press, 1978.
11. Gane, C. and Sarson, T. *Structured Systems Analysis: Tools and Techniques*. Englewood Cliffs NJ: Prentice-Hall, 1978.
12. Weinberg, V. *Structured Analysis*. New York: Yourdon Press, 1978.
13. *An Introduction to SADT*. SofTech Document 9022-78R, 1976.
14. Lippard, M.S. "Structured Methods: The Impossible Dream?" *Computerworld*, Vol. 14, No. 49 (December 1980) In Depth 1–15.
15. Brooks, F. *The Mythical Man-Month*. Reading MA: Addison-Wesley, 1975.
16. Henrotay, M. "Structured Revolution Continues—Large Organization Reports Success." *Futures*, (Fall 1979), 3–5.

Bibliography

Weinberg, G. *Rethinking Systems Analysis and Design*. Cambridge MA: Winthrop Publishers, forthcoming.

12 Protecting Proprietary Interests in Software

by Susan H. Nycum

INTRODUCTION

Protecting proprietary interests in software is a multifaceted task that requires knowledge in at least four areas:
- Corporate policy and the company business plan
- The structure and design of software
- Data processing security
- Intellectual property law

Few DP managers have all this expertise in-house, but all proprietors of software can and should add to their skills from outside sources.

Those involved with software—owners, users, OEMs, employees, and competitors—have two conflicting goals; sometimes the same party pursues both goals simultaneously for different products. One goal is to protect the software, either to ensure competitive advantage by preventing others from using the software or to charge for its use or disclosure. The other goal is to defeat protection so that the software can be used and transferred at will and without cost. The particular goal sought by an organization depends on the corporate business plan and policy; however, the DP manager should understand the boundaries of fair and legal business practice that apply to users and owners of software as well as to their competitors.

This chapter focuses on the legal aspects of proprietary protection of software, discussing the types of software, the goals of the involved parties, and the forms of legal protection available. The precautions the DP manager should take to avoid software-related legal problems are also discussed.

TYPES OF SOFTWARE

Before identifying the types of software involved, it is helpful to know why the laws differentiate software from other parts of computer systems. Software is a form of intellectual property (a valuable, intangible asset consisting of ideas, processes, and methods) that is relatively new and eludes analogy to previously existing products. Debate continues as to whether software is a product, a technical process, or a professional service. Software is thus unique as a subject of treatment under existing law, and applying the law requires adapting current legal concepts to particular forms of software. The following paragraphs define the four types of software that are considered for proprietary protection.

Traditional Software. This category includes software (such as operating systems) developed to run on specific machines as well as machine-independent software (such as application programs). The software may be in source (human-readable) form or object (machine-readable) form. Some software is easily translated into a different programming language or converted to run on a different CPU.

Firmware. This is hardware with programs. Firmware is not reprogrammable—it can be changed only by physical or mechanical modification or by replacement of components. Firmware is not usually accessible for reloading by the user.

Chip Technology. Like hardware, chip technology is tangible, but a chip may be classified with software if the process or direction to operate the device is part of the chip. A chip can be copied readily at low cost and can be reverse engineered. At present, chips cannot be encrypted to prevent reverse engineering.

Documentation. Some current definitions of software include the hardcopy documentation that accompanies the code, including systems documentation, user documentation, operator documentation, and sometimes the prompts and formats printed by the system on typewriter or CRT terminals.

FORMS OF LEGAL PROTECTION

There are currently five forms of legal protection that can apply to software:
- Patent
- Copyright
- Trade secret
- Trademark
- Contract

These forms of protection are discussed in detail in the following paragraphs.

Patent

Patent protection is a federal statutory right giving the inventor or his assignee exclusive rights to use or sell a product or process for 17 years from the effective filing date. An invention must meet several criteria to receive patent protection. First, it must involve statutory subject matter (i.e., physical methods, apparatus, compositions of matter, devices, and improvements). It cannot consist merely of an idea or a formula. Furthermore, the invention must be new, useful, not obvious, and must be described according to patent regulations in a properly filed and prosecuted patent application.

The status of patent protection for software in 1981 was ambiguous. In three rulings the U.S. Supreme Court has held particular pieces of software unpatentable because of failure to meet one or more of the tests described previously. The Court has declined to patent what it felt was merely a formula[1], it has held a process nonpatentable for obviousness [2], and it has refused a patent when the only novelty involved was the form of carrying out a nonpatentable step.

More recently, the Supreme Court has handed down two decisions that may have some effect on future patentability claims. These cases involve programs that are part of inventions otherwise eligible for patent. In one case, the Court decided that a process control application for curing synthetic rubber should not be denied a patent simply because it uses an algorithm and a computer [3]. The U.S. Patent Office must still determine whether the entire process is novel enough to warrant a patent.

In a companion case, the Court let stand a lower court ruling [4] that a module of the Honeywell Series 60 Level 64 computer system should be considered for patent. The module, which includes hardware and firmware, is a storage and retrieval device using internal scratchpad registers. Again, the device must meet the novelty requirement before actually receiving a patent. It is stressed that these decisions involve software or firmware that is part of a patentable device or process; these decisions do not reverse past rulings that software itself is not patentable.

Even if there were a major change in software patent policy, few owners would seek patent status for their software. The patent process is lengthy and expensive and requires full disclosure of the idea. Furthermore, a patent has only a 50 percent chance of surviving a challenge to its validity in the courts. For those few programs that really do represent technological breakthroughs, however, a patent would provide the exclusive right to use or sell the program for 17 years (patents are nonrenewable).

Copyright

Copyright is the federal statutory protection for writings of an author. Writings created since January 1, 1978, are protected by the new copyright law, which provides exclusive rights to the author or his assignee for the copyright, publication, broadcast, translation, adaptation, display, and performance of the idea contained in the work from the time it is embodied in tangible form. This protection is lost if the writing is published without copyright notice, which consists of the word copyright (or ©), the date, and the author's name. This notice must be affixed so that it attracts the attention of third parties (e.g., on the first or inside front page of a book or pamphlet). In late 1980 a federal copyright bill was enacted to cover computer programs and data bases explicitly.

Copyright is inexpensive and can be obtained quickly. The notice must be placed on the tangible form of expression (e.g., a computer tape), and one required and one optional copy must be submitted to the copyright office along with minor filing fees. The required copy is placed in the Library of Congress. (Software, however, is exempt from this requirement.) The second copy can be the first and last 25 pages of the program in object (machine-readable) form. Although optional, the second copy is a prerequisite for bringing an infringement suit and for some remedies such as minimum damages and attorney fees. The copyright remains in effect for 50 years beyond the death of the author and is nonrenewable.

Because copyright protects only against copying and requires disclosure of the idea, its usefulness is limited for some programs. It can be adequate protection, however, for inexpensive package programs sold in the multiple copy market. The function of such programs is not unique; the value to the owner lies in selling thousands of copies.

Trade Secret

A trade secret is a right protected by state rather than federal law. It is defined in many states as a secret formula, pattern, scheme, or device used in the operation of a business that gives the organization a competitive advantage. Computer programs have qualified as trade secrets in a number of court cases [5, 6, 7].

The requirement for trade secret status is that the item must remain secret. Absolute secrecy is not required; for example, if the secret is disclosed only to people bound (by virtue of their relationship or by contract) to keep it confidential, trade secret status is maintained regardless of how many people know it. Confidential relationships include employees, agents in a fiduciary or trust relationship, and thieves. In order to prevent thieves from profiting from ill-gotten knowledge, the laws hold that they are in a constructive trust relationship. Thus, any profits gained from the use or disclosure of a stolen trade secret are forwardable to the state if the thief is caught.

Contract is used to bind licensees and joint venture partners or investors. In some states these people are bound even without contract.

Once the secret is disclosed without a requirement of confidentiality or is disclosed to someone who does not know its secret character, the trade secret status is lost forever. (Trade secrets are often disclosed carelessly to user groups and at technical meetings.) If the secret is not disclosed, however, the protection can last forever.

Employees who learn the secret in the course of their duties are bound not to misappropriate it because of their trust relationship. Many employees do not realize the comprehensive nature of that trust and should consult their lawyers before using software developed for an employer for their own purposes.

Trade secrets can also be lost through reverse engineering. Many software owners encrypt their code to prevent reverse engineering.

Trademark

Trademark protection provides the exclusive right to use a symbol to identify goods and services. Trademark rights take effect upon use. Registra-

PROPRIETARY INTERESTS

tion with the U.S. Patent Office or a state agency is not necessary to obtain trademark status, but it helps greatly in exercising trademark rights. Trademark protection exists at both the federal and state levels. The protected symbol can be both a trade name and a logo (e.g., AUERBACH Publishers Inc and ▲). The protection afforded by the trademark is limited to the name of the program—the code itself is not protected. Because the major benefit of trademark protection is to prevent another product from being given the same name, this protection is useful only for programs that will be marketed.

Contract

Copies of software are ordinarily transferred to others in the course of doing business (sometimes in source form); therefore, transfer is frequently accompanied by an agreement to keep the software confidential. Patented and copyrighted software can be transferred using contracts that have more restrictive provisions than the patent or copyright law requires. The owner can, for example, contract with another not to disclose a copyrighted piece of software. In addition, remedies for disclosure or unauthorized copying, complex formulas for royalty payment for legitimate use, and the ownership of enhancements and changes to the software can also be delineated in a contract.

SELECTING THE RIGHT PROTECTION

The type of protection that is best for a particular program depends on several factors:
1. The longer the lifespan of the program, the more likely it becomes that the expensive investment of patent protection will be worthwhile.
2. The higher the value of the program, the more money that can reasonably be spent on protection.
3. Algorithms that must be disclosed widely are (if otherwise worth the investment) best protected by patent, which precludes use as well as duplication. Copyright protects only against copying, and trade secret protection is lost forever if the algorithm is inadvertently disclosed outside a confidential relationship.
4. The most expensive protection is patent; the least expensive is copyright.
5. Patents take the longest time to obtain; the other forms offer almost immediate protection.
6. A patent protects against reverse engineering; trade secret protection is lost if the program can be reverse engineered.

These factors are summarized in Table 12-1.

Unresolved Legal Issues

Two unresolved but important legal issues affect this analysis. The first is the patentability of software discussed previously. The DP manager and corporate counsel should keep track of the continuing legal debate in this area. The second unresolved issue is the legal relationship between copyright and

Table 12-1. Decision Table for Types of Legal Protection

Decision Factor	High	Medium	Low
Estimated lifespan of the program	C or TS	P	C or TS
Value of the program to the owner	P, C, TS	P, C, TS	C, TS
Need to disclose the program to others	P, C	TS, C	TS
Owner's expense budget	P, TS, C	TS, C	C
Time sensitivity	TS, C	P, TS, C	P, TS
Susceptibility to reverse engineering	P	P, TS	TS, C

Notes:
C   Copyright
P   Patent
TS Trade secret

trade secret protection when both are used for the same product. Trade secret protection has been held by the U.S. Supreme Court to be compatible with patent protection [8], but the Court has yet to decide whether a trade secret can be copyrighted to protect the secret in case it is disclosed.

The policies underlying the two forms of protection conflict: federal copyright protection requires disclosure, while state trade secret protection involves a nondisclosure agreement. According to some legal scholars, a court could rule that a copyrighted program is not eligible for trade secret protection. Other legal scholars argue that since the disclosure requirement for federal patent protection has not preempted trade secret protection, the Supreme Court should also uphold the right of software owners to receive both trade secret and copyright protection.

Suggested Strategies

Because of these critical and unresolved legal issues, software developers should carefully evaluate the types of protection and remain alert to changes in the laws. At present, the best alternative is often to copyright software and then to license or disclose the software, using agreements that restrict use, transfer, and disclosure. This approach should not conflict with existing copyright law theory, and it achieves the same secrecy afforded by trade secret protection.

Embodying the program in firmware is another alternative that should be considered. Firmware cannot be altered by the user and inhibits copying and user enhancements. In addition, the recent Supreme Court decision suggests that firmware can receive patent protection if it is part of a patentable device. It should be remembered, however, that without patent protection, firmware is susceptible to reverse engineering and thus to loss of trade secret status.

EMPLOYER-EMPLOYEE RELATIONSHIPS

Many problems covering software protection arise from the employment relationship, where two philosophies often conflict. One philosophy is that the products of the employee belong to the employer; the other is that employees should be free to change jobs during their careers and to use the expertise gained in one job in new work situations.

Although some employers might argue that all work done during employment belongs to them, and some employees might claim that their creations are theirs exclusively, the laws do not generally support either claim. State laws vary on this question; however, the prevailing view is that programs written or developed as a specific task assigned by the employer belong exclusively to the employer and that programs written or developed solely by the employee, using the employee's own time and resources, belong exclusively to the employee. Most controversy over software ownership falls in the gray area between these two positions.

The following discussion centers on trade secret law since patent and copyright protection are less helpful. Patent protection for software is ambiguous and hence rarely used, and most companies have a well-established patent assignment policy. On the other hand, the new copyright law is explicit regarding work for hire:

> In the case of a work made for hire, the employer or other person for whom the work was prepared is considered the author for purposes of this title, and, unless the parties have expressly agreed otherwise in a written instrument signed by them, owns all of the rights comprised in the copyright [9].

Trade secret ownership conflicts between employers and employees for other than assigned work are usually resolved based on the resources used. Employees who develop new software on their own time, at home, on a personally owned terminal, but using employer computer time, may be found to own the program; however, the employer may be given a royalty-free license to use the program in its business. A more complex question concerns employees working at home on flextime or with an employer-owned terminal or microcomputer. In such cases, proof of whose resources are used in development is more difficult to establish.

Software Ownership Policy

Legal battles over program ownership are very costly to both sides and consume enormous amounts of time and energy. Often a court "divides the baby" so that neither side actually wins. To avoid going to court over program ownership, employers should have an explicit policy regarding employee-developed programs. This policy can be part of an organization-wide trade secret protection plan developed by management and legal counsel.

Each employee involved in developing software should be required to sign an agreement concerning ownership of software at the time of hire. A formal employment or secrecy agreement or an informal letter to the employer can be used. Since both types of agreements are legally effective, management style should determine which approach is used. The informal letter is friendlier, but the awesome contract form may make a more lasting impression on the employee.

If a simple letter is used, the following format is recommended for the key paragraph:

> All computer programs written by me, either alone or with others, during the period of my employment, commencing on _____, 19___, and up to and including a period of _____ after termination, whether or not conceived or made during my regular working hours, are the sole property of the company.

Such an agreement prevents misunderstanding and protects the employer against legal action.

Departing Employees

Employees may use skills developed during previous jobs; however, they may not use trade secrets disclosed to or produced by them during those jobs. This is enjoinable behavior and may result in the award of damages to the former employer. Departing employees should take nothing tangible from the old job—listings, notebooks, tapes, documents, or copies of any kind, including lists of specific customers. Prospective employers should carefully avoid crossing the fine line between hiring someone to provide expertise in a particular area and hiring someone to provide knowledge of a competitor's proprietary products or business plan. Special care is required when more than one employee is hired from the same company. (A California Supreme Court case describes what not to do [10].)

Departing employees should be reminded during the exit interview that no materials or proprietary concepts received during employment can be used at the new job. They should be asked to read and sign a statement that acknowledges their understanding of this point. The statement should also affirm that no materials have been removed from the employer's premises and that all those previously in the employee's possession have been returned. Employers should obtain the employee's new address in case later contact is necessary.

During the exit interview, employees should have the opportunity to clarify gray areas—programs they wrote on their own time using company terminals and company computer time, innovations they developed that the company never used, and so on. Permitting a departing employee to use an invention that will not cause loss of competitive advantage can ensure a friendly and loyal colleague in the marketplace. In any case, legal counsel should be involved in these sessions because an attorney experienced in trade secret law can interpret the nuances of the interview more effectively and can emphasize the consequences of unfair competitive conduct.

GUIDELINES FOR SOFTWARE USERS

Users who obtain software outside of contractual or other confidential relationships that preclude competitive action can legally reverse engineer the

PROPRIETARY INTERESTS

software and use it freely, even if they know it is a trade secret. In addition, users who obtain software from third parties without any knowledge that it is proprietary are free to use it. In such cases the third party may be liable to the owner for misappropriation. Software users should note, however, that *intentional* wrongful use in this situation may lead to criminal and civil liability for infringement or misappropriation.

Patented inventions can only be used with the owner's permission. The alleged infringer, however, can challenge the validity of the patent in court and, if successful, can defeat the patentee's exclusive right to use the invention.

Another problem concerns the ownership of a user-made change or enhancement that significantly alters the constitution of the software. Neither copyright nor trade secret law is explicit on this point, and ownership is commonly specified by contract. Many vendor-user agreements require the user to return all copies of the software at the end of the term; however, few vendors forbid user changes and enhancements or ask for royalties from new works embodying or based on their software. Some agreements contain provisions that any and all changes belong to the vendor. Thus, the software user should pay special attention to contract provisions regarding changes and enhancements.

In the absence of a specific agreement, the user takes some risk but has a fair chance of surviving a challenge that user-made changes infringe the vendor's rights.

CONCLUSION

The DP manager should understand the legal alternatives for protecting software. If the organization uses software developed and owned by outside parties, this understanding can prevent legal problems and can ensure that the terms of the agreement for using the software are proper. For organizations that develop software in-house, a corporate policy based on a thorough knowledge of the laws can prevent misunderstandings between management and development personnel. Such a policy can also ensure that the company does not lose competitive advantage because of unauthorized disclosure or copying of programs. Because the laws in this area are subject to change, the DP manager should consult legal counsel to keep pace with the latest developments.

References

The following references are in legal format to assist corporate counsel in further research.

1. Gottschalk v. Benson, 409 U.S. 63 (1972).
2. Dann v. Johnston, 425 U.S. 219 (1976).
3. Diamond v. Diehr and Lutton, 49 LW 4194 (1981).
4. In re Bradley and Franklin, 600 F. 2d 807 (C.C.P.A. 1979).
5. Com-Share Inc v. Computer Complex Inc, 338 F. Supp. 1229 (E.D. MI, 1971).
6. MSA v. Cyborg Systems Inc, 6 CLSR 921 (ND IL, 1978).
7. University Computing Corp v. Lykes-Youngstown Corp, 504 F. 2d 518 (5th Cir. 1974).
8. Kewanee Oil Co v. Bicron Corp, 416 U.S. 470 (1974).
9. 17 U.S.C. 202(b).
10. Bancroft-Whitney Co v. Glen, 64 C2d 327 (1966).

Bibliography

Parker v. Flook, 437 U.S. 584 (1978).

13 Security

by Jagdish R. Dalal

INTRODUCTION

Computer security involves technological and procedural safeguards for computer hardware, software, and data; the closely related field of computer privacy involves the protection of data from unauthorized access and/or alteration. In both cases, ethical, legal, and business issues are at stake.

When computer technology was young, computer security was a concern primarily for computer sites that processed or stored national security data. At that time, the methods of protecting information were simpler; physical security was the main concern. During the past decade, the technology supporting the information industry has created new situations and capabilities, and the complexities of security programs have increased greatly. The introduction of sophisticated software has increased the need for security measures other than physical protection. For example, in a multiprogramming environment, programs running simultaneously must be secured from one another.

Another technological advance that has increased the complexity of security programs, especially in a distributed environment, is the troduction of mini- and microprocessors. Distributed DP has increased access to data and in many instances has reduced the effectiveness of centralized organizational control. Distributed processors are usually connected by telecommunications links that further weaken security if adequate precautions are not observed.

Legislative Considerations

The increased use of computers by government agencies and private organizations to collect information about individuals has contributed to the concern about invasion of privacy. Coupled with the increased concern about the control of computing resources, computer security has become a primary issue for both DP managers and legislators.

To protect the privacy of individuals, Congress passed the Fair Credit Reporting Act of 1971, which established stringent regulations for credit-reporting agencies. Three years later, Congress passed the Privacy Act of 1974, which applies to federal agencies and their contractors. Many states have since enacted similar legislation regulating state (and sometimes local) governments. In 1978, the Office of Management and Budget issued Circular No. A-71 to both the heads of federal agencies and their contractors, thus establishing requirements for the security of automated information systems. This type of legislation, along with the public's heightened interest in protecting individual privacy, has contributed to growing awareness in protecting computers and computerized data.

ORGANIZING FOR SECURITY

Computer system security often requires organizational changes. If an effective security program is to be established, organizational and administrative controls must be developed and implemented. Before establishing a security program, planners must develop a description of potential exposures, including the adverse effects each exposure might have on the DP organization. This list of exposures can be used as a checklist in developing a security plan.

The old Army expression, "Security is everyone's business," is appropriate here. The need for security must be understood by the entire organization, not only by the security officer or DP manager. Even though the security of a DP organization is the responsibility of the DP manager, a security organization should be established and headed by a computer security program manager. Depending on the organization's size, the position of security manager can be either full- or part-time. In any case, one individual must be aware of changes in security requirements and must lead the effort to establish a coordinated security program. Figure 13-1 depicts an organizational chart that can be adapted to a DP security program, identifying the functions of the program. These functions are not necessarily full-time positions.

Administrative Safeguards

Before completing a security program, planners must develop and implement administrative safeguards, including policies, procedures, and standards. The employee in charge of administrative security safeguards should develop control functions that can serve as a basis for security policies and procedures. Four areas in which control functions are necessary are:
- Identification of threats
- Protection from loss
- Detection methods that can minimize loss when accidents, disasters, or security violations occur
- Recovery methods and steps that can prevent future losses

Control procedures vary from organization to organization according to the scope of the security program and the associated risk analysis. Typical control procedures include:
- Establishing formal security procedures and periodic reviews of compliance
- Establishing progress reviews and analyses (e.g., security walk-throughs during systems development phases)

SECURITY

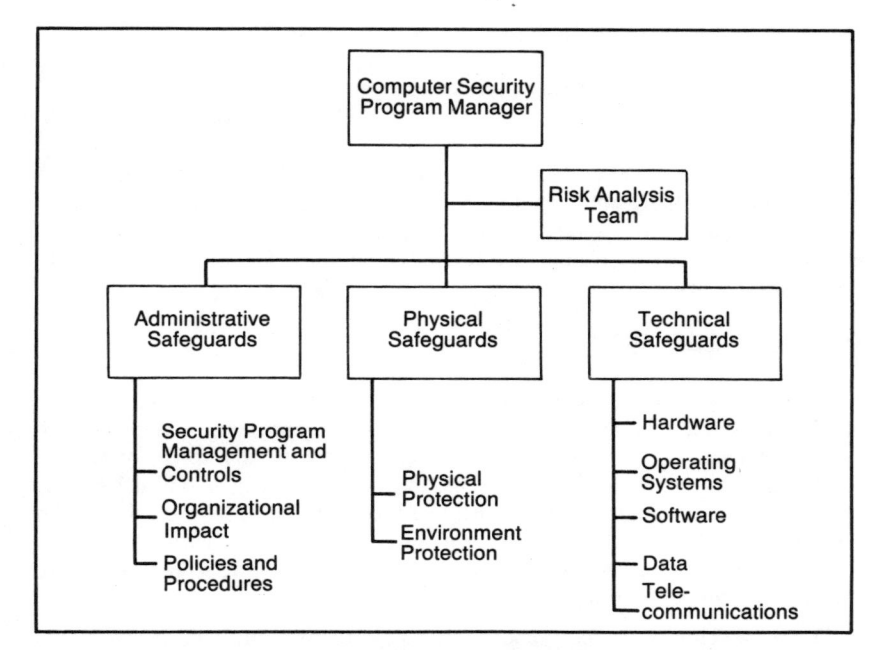

Figure 13-1. Computer Security Organization Functions

- Establishing formal communication channels for monitoring adherence to security procedures
- Periodically evaluating the entire security program

These control procedures are crucial to an effective security program, especially in a quickly changing or high-risk environment.

Organizational Impact

Implementation of a security program affects the entire organization. Some changes are desirable; others, however, can be detrimental to overall security or to the entire organization.

Three areas of organizational impact should be reviewed and monitored:
- Awareness and education
- Attitude
- Personnel selection and assignment

Personnel selection and assignment is generally regarded as the most critical area. Such factors as background checks and separation of duties are important. However, even with proper personnel selection and assignment, a security program can fail if employees are unaware of or uneducated about the need to maintain security. An ongoing awareness and education program must be instituted and updated frequently to reflect the latest changes in the organization's DP environment. Employee attitude is another important security consideration. Employee dissatisfaction often results in shoddy work habits that can destroy the effectiveness of even the best security measures.

Policies and Procedures

Computer system protection policies and procedures are designed to meet various objectives. In general, however, the policies provide direction, standards, goals, and definitions that require good judgment and discretion. The procedures provide documentation and instructions on how to meet the goals set forth in the policies and are intended to ensure a high degree of uniformity in job performance. A well-prepared policies and procedures manual can act as an effective control in itself and facilitate development of a structured, coordinated security program.

PHYSICAL SECURITY

Physical security measures are intended to reduce or prevent disruption of service, loss of assets, and unauthorized access to equipment. In many organizations, because of growing dependence on computers, disruption of service can be devastating. Unauthorized access to information can also affect service by reducing confidence in the security of the information. Unless computer equipment is rendered physically secure, any attempts to protect the system and data will be futile. Thus, physical security is the first issue to be considered when developing a security program.

When developing a comprehensive, cost-effective physical security program, management must thoroughly analyze the computer operation. Involving the equipment insurance carrier in this analysis can contribute to a more comprehensive security program. The following steps should be considered by management:
- Review and identify assets.
- Identify threats to the security of assets.
- Determine the effect these threats might have.
- Perform a risk analysis.
- Develop countermeasures.
- Identify and minimize exposures and/or shortcomings.
- Implement a plan for countermeasures.

Identifying threats and developing countermeasures requires a thorough knowledge of the characteristics of the DP installation and the entire organization. Therefore, suggestions from other departments of the organization (or subscribers to the computer service) can contribute to the security analysis.

Threats to Physical Security

Threats can arise from environmental hazards or from human action and can either destroy or improperly modify the functioning of the system. Environmental hazards can often have unpredictable and far-reaching impact. If unanticipated and if no disaster recovery plan is initiated, these hazards can cripple the organization. Human destruction of equipment or data is usually easier to contain. These damaging acts originate from many sources, ranging from sabotage to inadvertent errors in employee judgment.

SECURITY

When designing a physical security program, the planner should consider the potential threats listed in Figure 13-2 and plan countermeasures for them. The list is only a guide and is not intended to be comprehensive. The unexpected threat is often the most difficult to handle. Therefore, all possible occurrences, regardless of their unusual nature, should be investigated. The probability of a plane crashing into the data center might be slim, but if the building is located on a regular flight path, the type of damage that could be caused by a crash should be investigated.

Threats	a	b	c	d	e	f	g	h	i	j	k	l	m
Environmental Hazards													
• Fire	x	x	x	x	x		x					x	x
• Earthquake	x	x		x	x		x					x	
• Severe Storms	x	x		x	x		x					x	
• Flooding	x	x		x	x		x					x	
• Power Brownouts or Failures			x	x		x							
• Air Conditioning Failures				x		x							
Human Destruction													
• Malicious Damage	x	x	x	x	x	x		x	x	x			x
• Fraud								x		x	x	x	x
• Embezzlement								x		x	x	x	x
• Theft			x		x			x	x	x	x	x	x
• Unauthorized Use of Facilities			x		x			x	x	x	x	x	x
• Sabotage/Espionage			x	x	x			x		x	x	x	x
• Inadvertent Destruction				x							x	x	x

Countermeasures Key:
a. Building design
b. Building operation
c. Placement of detection devices
d. Identification and testing of backup facilities
e. Fire/police notification system
f. Backup power/air conditioning sources
g. Access to weather forecasts
h. System access control
i. Secured doors and windows
j. Personnel screening program
k. Strict adherence to audit trails, logging facilities, and control procedures
l. Well-documented standards and procedures
m. Personnel education/awareness training

Figure 13-2. Threats and Countermeasures

Hardware Security

Some physical security countermeasures considered in the preceding list can also serve to protect hardware. In many instances, however, these countermeasures are inadequate protection against unauthorized access because the perpetrator may already have physical access to the system. Developing a good security program for hardware protection again requires considering possible threats, divided as follows:
- Disruption of service
- Theft or disclosure of information
- Unauthorized alteration of information
- Destruction of information

Threats against hardware security are often more difficult to identify and quantify than are threats to physical security. The following list includes some possible countermeasures:
- Memory protection
- Execution protection
- I/O processing protection
- Hard and soft access control
- Cryptography (for communications)
- Well-documented systems and procedures
- Predefined scheduling and adherence to procedures

Many of these countermeasures require additional capabilities from the operating system and greater technical knowledge about the operation of the system and programs. Security problems associated with data transmission are complex, and countermeasures in this area are therefore harder to implement. For example, cryptographic technology ranges from simple algorithmic encryption of messages to complex hardware- and software-oriented cryptography devices. Using these devices involves significant planning and requires changes in the day-to-day operation of the computer installation.

OPERATING SYSTEM SECURITY

Physical security and hardware security cannot provide an impenetrable environment unless the operating system that manages the computer resources and enforces the controls on both computer and data resources is also secure. Some of today's operating systems have functions that help to secure the systems themselves. The following list includes some of these features:
- Isolation of processes in virtual machine systems such as VM/370
- Isolation of second-level operating systems, as in VM/370 and MVS
- Single-source job scheduling, as in the job entry scheduling (JES) facility of OS/VS1
- Primary and secondary spooling of all devices
- Automatic error recovery and logging in case of hardware or software failure
- Spooling and logging capabilities of communication lines and messages
- Console and/or display lockout features
- Password protection features
- Detailed and accurate job accounting, including various counts of I/O transactions, as in the system management facility (SMF) of OS/VS1
- Simplified user-oriented command languages, as in the query-by-example (QBE) facility available from IBM Corporation

The aforementioned are only a few of the major operating system features that help in a security program. These and other features, however, contribute to the complexity of the operating system, rendering specifications for the development of the operating system and related software complex and voluminous. To establish the security control features of the operating system, one must verify these specifications to ensure that the operating system and application software meet the original objectives and that the controls required for the security program are uncompromising. Several verification techniques are included in the following sections.

Desk Checking. A rather tedious method, desk checking compares the operating system code with the security program's specifications and control requirements. Because of the complexity of today's operating systems and associated logistical problems, this process is seldom used.

Penetration Tests. Computer security experts are given access to the system and to the design and program documentation. These experts then attempt to penetrate the system or various subsystems, identifying weak spots in the process. Since these penetration tests are hit or miss, confidence in the results depends on the extent of the tests performed and the expertise of the personnel performing them.

Kernel Method. With this method, experts identify a "kernel" of the operating system that controls the security features. This new approach is gaining in popularity, especially in large computer installations that store national security information. Users of the kernel method attempt to isolate certain rudiments essential to the functioning of the operating system. By implementing these rudiments in software and verifying them thoroughly, users of this method believe that they can guarantee the security of the total system. Critics point out, however, that the identification and construction of the kernel is difficult and beyond the resources of most computer installations. Ford Aerospace and Communications Corporation, a subsidiary of Ford Motor Company, has developed a Kernelized Secure Operating System (KSOS) that is considered a major achievement in this area.

In summary, the protection of the operating system as well as the security provided by the operating system are the weakest links in current security programs. Until security is considered an inherent capability of an operating system, we will continue to hear about such security problems as the precocious college student who adjusts the grading software of his school's computer system.

SOFTWARE SECURITY

Two aspects of software security are addressed here: software development security and data security.

Software Development Security

If security is to be a major consideration in an application, security control features must be considered from the beginning of the system development life cycle. The complexity of interaction in the system, subsystem, and program modules makes retrofitting control features a time-consuming and expensive task. Therefore, control features and security considerations should be built into the software as part of the initial design.

The typical system development process consists of the following phases:
- Project initiation and initial survey
- Cost/benefit analysis
- In-depth study and business system design
- Computer system design
- Programming
- System test and conversion
- System installation
- Post-installation reviews

Control features and security requirements are associated with each phase. When considered as part of the system design methodology, these features can help produce a secure system. The following sections discuss the security considerations for each system development phase.

Project Initiation and Initial Survey. As data is gathered to identify the uses of the proposed system, planners should also identify control features and security requirements. For example, when developing a human resource information system, planners should identify potentially private information and possible access control features.

Cost/Benefit Analysis. During this phase, the security risk analysis should be performed to quantify overall security requirements, threats, and countermeasures. The cost/benefit study must include the results of the security risk analysis study. For example, a cost/benefit analysis for an electronic funds transfer system (EFTS) that did not include considerations of security and control features would overlook an expensive segment of the system.

In-Depth Study and Business System Design. Overall software requirements are determined and total specifications developed during this phase. Security control features should be included as part of the business system design. For example, when developing an accounts payable system, one should identify such control features as batch totaling and hash controls.

Computer System Design. Such additional controls as password protection of data and key number validation are identified and included in programming specifications during the computer system design phase.

Programming. During this mechanical phase of program development, specifications developed in earlier phases (including security features) are coded.

System Test and Conversion. Security and control features are tested in a systems environment and validated for accuracy and effectiveness during this phase. If the controls are found inadequate, they must be tightened up before the system is turned over to the user for operation. The conversion plan is also tested for adequacy and effectiveness of the controls to be used during the conversion phase.

SECURITY 165

System Installation. The system is installed in a full operating environment in this phase. The control features are retested for accuracy and effectiveness.

Post-Installation Reviews. All systems should undergo post-installation reviews to determine the currency of software, applicability of the software to the current environment, and continued effectiveness of the control features.

Throughout the system development process, extensive documentation should be developed. The documentation should be used in developing operating instructions and procedures. As discussed previously, documentation in itself is a countermeasure against certain threats to the computer system.

Data Security

In most instances, confidentiality and credibility of information is the heart of the computer security program. If the managers of a computer installation cannot guarantee the integrity and safety of information, users will be reluctant to subscribe to the services.

Most modern data base management systems make allowances for the security of stored information. It is the DP manager's responsibility, however, to ensure data security. The following points are guidelines for providing such protection:
- When acquiring a data base management system, the procurement specifications should include criteria for providing data security.
- When developing new software that utilizes data bases, the programming specifications must delineate controls and access protection methodology. These specifications must again be tested for adequacy before the system becomes operational.
- During the application development process, user involvement should be sought in designing data security measures.
- Equal attention should be paid to ensuring data integrity and to preventing unauthorized access to data.

Levels of Control

Unauthorized use of a data base can be prevented by imposing controls at several points. Many of these controls are similar to other security measures discussed in this chapter:
- Access to data should be controlled by physical security measures. Data file sources (e.g., a tape library) should be physically separate from access mechanisms (e.g., terminals).
- Application programs should be logged in properly, using electronically or manually recorded information (e.g., job setup sheets for batch jobs or automatic logging by online operating systems).
- Especially sensitive data should be protected by operating system features as well as by a data base management system with multiple levels of password protection. The various passwords must remain confiden-

tial and be changed periodically.
- System and data base documentation should list (preferably by name but at least by position) those employees authorized to access information, and the documentation itself must be protected.

Additional Considerations

Many of today's data base management systems do not provide substantial protection against unauthorized access of data. The controls (usually password oriented) are primitive and consume excessive computing resources. Because of their shortcomings, these basic precautions are often bypassed by application software, and inadequate security is provided. When required, a control program can be developed, either as a superset of or in conjunction with the data base, to provide additional control and logging features. These programs can be developed without taxing other resources.

Regardless of the type of controls developed, total security can never be achieved. Even the best controls only provide a defense that is difficult (although not impossible) to penetrate. Therefore, constant vigilance must be maintained, and controls must be reviewed periodically to maintain the defenses.

RISK ANALYSIS

The common objective of most risk assessment strategies is to produce a quantitative analysis of risks and a financial justification for countermeasures. To develop an effective security program, it is necessary to assess the probability of occurrence for each threat and determine the cost of implementing countermeasures. Threat probability is an important yet often neglected element of calculation. For example, if a data center in Florida develops a set of countermeasures for the threat of snowstorms without considering the probability of a snowstorm occurring, the countermeasures will probably be uneconomical. Although risk analysis requires mathematical formulation, intuition can play a part. To perform objective trade-off studies, however, one must quantify as many factors as possible. The following discussion of risk analysis applies, regardless of whether the factors are quantified.

Risk Analysis Methodology

The risk analysis methodology used for the security program should resemble other corporate methodologies and monetary guidelines used to protect assets. Figure 13-3 depicts the necessary steps in developing a risk analysis.

The risk analysis program methodology consists of two major considerations:
- Since the risk analysis is presented as a mathematical cost/benefit analysis, such numerical values as probabilities, value of loss, and cost should be well thought-out and consistent. In establishing the precise monetary expense of a loss, a tendency often exists to minimize the

SECURITY

expense while exaggerating the cost of implementing countermeasures. To realistically assess threats, countermeasures, and reasonable cost/value estimates, a risk analysis team should be established, composed of representatives from DP management, security, key user organizations (or clients), and the financial staff. Since team members can also act as control monitors for the security program, the team should receive permanent status.
* No security program is ever complete; its effectiveness must be continually evaluated. Evaluation can serve as a feedback loop when performing future risk analyses.

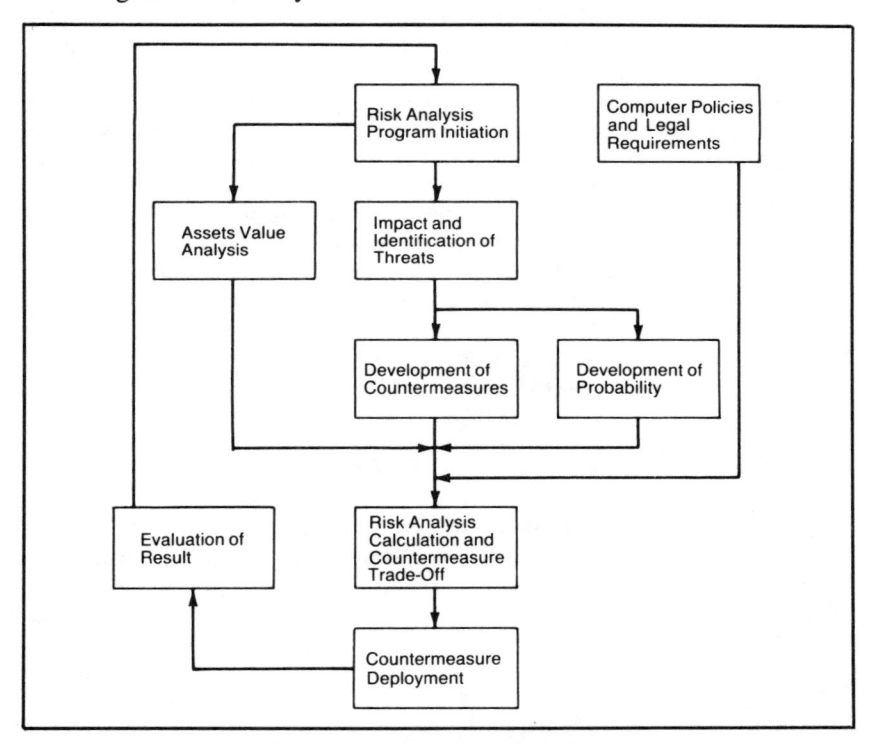

Figure 13-3. Risk Analysis Methodology

CONTINGENCY PLANNING

Even with a thoughtfully constructed security plan, a corporation might encounter a situation in which it must abandon its primary processing installation and rely on a backup site. Such a disruption in service can result from fire, storm, vandalism, or power failure and can last for one day or for weeks. Careful planning can reduce the losses incurred by such a disaster. Unfortunately, many contingency plans are insufficiently developed. A comprehensive plan can greatly assist management in coping with such disruptions. A typical contingency plan should include at least the following:

- Emergency notification procedure—Procedures for notifying appropriate personnel of an emergency should specify the initial steps required in the absence of those authorities usually responsible for emergency procedures.
- Contingency organization list—The names and specific responsibilities of individuals in case of an emergency should be listed. Clear delineation of responsibility avoids wasting time in defining authority when the emergency arises.
- Identification of resources involved—All hardware and software resources must be itemized and documented, and the most recent levels to be recreated should be identified.
- List of available resources—A list of available backup resources (within a reasonable distance) should include the names of contacts for initiating emergency processing. This list must be updated periodically to reflect changes in hardware/software configuration and in the availability of backup facilities. The list should also include information about the compatibility of backup facilities.
- Written procedures and guidelines—A comprehensive set of procedures and guidelines must be developed in advance and documented to guide the emergency recovery team. Lack of definitions and clear instructions can significantly hamper the recovery process. These procedures and guidelines should also be updated as required.

The importance of maintaining current contingency plans cannot be emphasized enough. Although it is hoped that these plans will never be needed, they are an essential part of DP management.

THE FUTURE OF COMPUTER SECURITY

With the ever-increasing demands on computer installations to protect information, computer system security will increasingly concern DP managers. The introduction of more sophisticated hardware and software will probably complicate security issues; however, it is hoped that more hardware and software manufacturers will incorporate security measures into their product designs. Additional governmental legislation is required to guide legal authorities in the issue of computer crime. More formal education is needed to help train future security officers and DP managers in security methods.

CONCLUSION

Computer security and privacy encompass a broad range of problems that complicate the implementation of security measures. The most critical elements in a security program are an awareness of the importance of security and a willingness on the part of DP management to confront the task. The control features of any security program are useless if the people effecting the controls do not understand security requirements and are not convinced of the value of the program.